DEBT-FREE LIVING

Debt-Free Living

LARRY BURKETT AND KEITH TONDEUR

MONARCH

Crowborough

British Library Cataloguing Data
A catalogue record for this book is available
from the British Library.

ISBN 1 85424 367 5

Designed and produced by Bookprint Creative Services
P.O. Box 827, BN21 3YJ, England for
MONARCH PUBLICATIONS
Broadway House, The Broadway
Crowborough, East Sussex, TN6 1HQ.
Printed in Great Britain.

CONTENTS

ACKNOWLEDGEMENTS

First, I would like to thank Larry Burkett for giving me the opportunity of working with him on this book. I regard Larry as the leading Christian teacher in the area of money so I feel very honoured to have been invited to write this book with him. I am also extremely grateful to Andrew Buchanan-Smith of the Speakeasy Advice Centre and Mike Reeves of Debt Solutions for writing the appendices on Benefits and Bankruptcy which I am sure will prove invaluable to many readers. My thanks to Liz Lown who has had an even more difficult job than usual in combining two texts and two different forms of English. Thank you all very much.

DISCLAIMER

Because of the nature of this book, simplifications and generalisations have had to be made. Dealing with debt is often extremely complicated and therefore we cannot be held responsible for any action taken, or indeed not taken, by readers based solely on the contents of this book. Anyone facing serious debt problems must seek expert advice.

Useful addresses

Credit Action
6 Regent Terrace
CAMBRIDGE
CB2 1AA

Debt Solutions
Havering Grange Centre
Havering Road
ROMFORD
RM1 4HR

Speakeasy Advice Centre
4 Arabella Street
Roth
CARDIFF
CF2 4TA

INTRODUCTION

Of all the problems facing families and individuals in the 1990s none is more distressing than debt. The first thing that must be said is that there is a difference between credit and debt. Credit, which in itself is not necessarily bad, is merely a temporary extension of one's income-earning ability. Debt is an over extension of this process. It usually carries with it an unrealistic presumption about future earnings. When you buy things on credit that you cannot afford to own, you do not avoid the consequences, you simply delay them and often make them much worse. Too often credit is used to delay making initial decisions until it is far too late. An example of this is when a newly married couple buy a house where making the monthly payments is dependent upon 'ideal' circumstances – i.e. two incomes with uninterrupted earnings and often overtime as well. Thus even normal events such as pregnancy or illness can plunge people quickly into unmanageable debt.

When someone gets into debt through indulgence and greed, it is often not the result of a conscious decision. It is the result of decisions clouded by good intentions and rationalisations. For some, the worst thing that could happen is for them to achieve all their financial goals as they are then able to surround themselves with so many 'things' that they can try to avoid facing up to the reality of how miserable they really are. If you find this hard to believe, then just think for a moment of the number of stories you have read about the 'upwardly mobile' who get caught up in the excesses of alcohol and/or drugs in an attempt to escape from the shallowness of their lives.

There is a predictable cycle whenever someone gets into debt. The first phase is denial. The problem is ignored in the hope that it will somehow magically cure itself. At this stage one partner will often subconsciously, or consciously, blame the other for the problem. The next phase is fear and frustration when the creditors begin to harass through letters or phone calls. This will often stir up enough stress to motivate people to the next step – taking out a debt consolidation loan. Thus most of the accumulated and unsecured debts will be put into one debt repayment which is usually secured against one's home. This often leads to a slightly reduced payment and thus in the short-term pressures may ease somewhat. However, unfortunately, within a few months most people still find themselves in even bigger debt because they have continued to overspend, often using the previous paid-off credit cards and thus have extra payments to make.

Sadly, the actual pressure of debt can make someone go out and buy something new like a car. In our society the ability to buy new things is often equated with self-worth, so a big purchase gives a short-term 'pick-me-up'. But obviously this only compounds the problems. So in desperation people try to find a radical solution – divorce and bankruptcy leading the list. But as these are attempts to avoid the problem rather than deal with it, these 'solutions' will not work either. Many who divorce or go bankrupt because of financial problems will repeat their mistakes later in life.

The reason that most of these 'solutions' don't work is that they aren't really solutions, they merely treat the symptoms. The symptoms are what you see – overdue bills, indulgences, too many credit cards, too large houses etc. The problems are primarily ignorance and attitude.

It is an indictment on both our education system and our homes that people can even leave university with no basic understanding of how to manage money sensibly. In fact you can graduate with a PhD in mathematics and still not know how to balance a cheque book.

Starting out debt-free is unlikely if you are buying a home, or if you have recently finished college, but if you are willing to follow some basic unchanging principles that have worked well for centuries, you can become debt-free.

We need to remember that nothing in the area of finances has so dominated or influenced the direction of our society during the last fifty years than debt. It's amazing when you consider that only a generation ago credit cards were unknown, car loans were a rarity and mortgages were for a very few. No one in our fathers' or grandfathers' generation would have believed that any banker would be so foolish as to lend a teenager money to go to college. Their advice would have been (and was) to 'Get a job'.

Today it is not unusual for a young couple to owe nearly £100,000 within the first two years of marriage. A profile of a young couple's debt often reveals their financial training – or lack of it – including a home mortgage of approximately £65,000, college loans (his and hers) £10,000, car loans (his and hers) £13,000. Often the list extends even further to include consolidation loans, finance company loans and parental loans. And why not? If it's good enough for the country, it's good enough for the family, right?

Christians would obviously say no, not necessarily. We're supposed to take our direction from God's word, not from the world. So the logical decision would be to observe what the church is doing and use that as our guide. However, in doing so, we will find that the average British churchgoer is as deeply in debt as any other member of our society, and with about the same rate of bad debts and bankruptcies.

The only reliable source of wisdom is the word of God itself. Only by going back to the true source of all wisdom can we possibly hope to find the right balance today. God's word tells us that his plan for us is to be debt-free. And even better, that we would be lenders rather than borrowers. Read Deuteronomy 28:12, 'The Lord will open the heavens, the storehouse of his bounty, to send rain on your land in season and to bless all the work of your hands. You will lend to many nations but will borrow from none'.

We hope to show that that is still God's plan and that it is entirely possible, even in this present generation. The blessings of becoming debt-free go far beyond the financial area. They extend to the spiritual and marital realms as well. No one who is financially bound can be spiritually free. The problems must certainly spill over into your prayer and study time. The effects of financial bondage on a marriage relationship are measurable in the statistics of failed marriages. Approximately forty per cent of all first marriages fail, and finances are listed as the leading cause of divorce by a factor of nearly four to one over any other cause, including fidelity.

We hope that if you're reading this book and aren't in debt yourself, you are doing so to help others who are in debt. If they are family members, especially grown-up children, we trust you will find this book a light in the darkness. We know of nothing more emotionally defeating for parents than to watch their children make financial mistakes repeatedly, while depending on their parents to bail them out of crisis after crisis. More money won't solve their problems. The old adage is 'more money in, more money out'. What is needed is a plan to help establish some financial discipline in their children's lives.

If you happen to be reading this book because a friend, a family member, or a counsellor recommended it to you, we trust that you will reserve judgement until you have read enough to understand the concepts presented. It is not our purpose to condemn or accuse anyone. We all have weaknesses that cause difficulties in our lives. Yours may be in the area of finances, whereas ours may be in other areas. We don't pretend to have all the answers, but we believe that God's word does, so we'll limit most of our advice to those areas that can be dealt with from his word.

In this book we will look into the lives of some people who ignored these biblical truths and predictably wound up deeply in debt. They made the decision to break free from the cycle that entrapped them and as a result all became totally debt-free.

We live in an economy that encourages the misuse of credit and then inflicts severe penalties on those who do misuse it. If you don't believe that is true, just talk to anyone who is struggling to repay loans offered so freely by lenders. Their attitudes can so easily change when they don't get their payment on time.

We pray that this book will put you on the road to financial success and a debt-free lifestyle and help you to escape from the fear and heartache that the slavery of debt causes for so many.

CHAPTER 1

A NATIONAL POLICY OF GROWTH THROUGH DEBT

If you were born after 1960 you don't remember when home mortgages were rare and car loans were for twelve months or less. Prior to that time the local bank manager was considered the most conservative businessman in town. If someone was approved for a loan, it was generally accepted that he was good for the money. The only regular line of credit most people had was from the local butcher or grocer, and those loans were based on honesty and dependability.

During the sixties an increasing number of people went off to college and millions more borrowed money to build homes and start businesses. The great credit boom of the twentieth century was up and running. Never before in history had our government used tax-generated money to support private lending, but the British people supported the idea wholeheartedly and a new idea was born – consumer credit.

With the stimulus of credit feeding the education, housing and business sectors, prices went up – the natural outgrowth of the law of supply and demand. Credit allowed more people to compete for the available products and services, which in turn allowed prices to increase. Once the cycle began, others were forced to borrow to compete for those items and private lenders stepped in to provide the loans. The boom of home loans in the sixties provided better housing to young couples

15

at a much earlier age then they could have ever realised by saving to buy their homes.

But there was a price to be paid, and that price was inflation. House prices began to creep up in the late sixties as more and more families entered the market through a wide variety of mortgage options. But as prices climbed, many couples were forced out of the market because they could not afford the monthly payments.

By the mid-seventies the generation of bankers who had been through the Depression had retired and operations were turned over to younger, more aggressive people who had grown up with the debt-oriented mentality. The need to expand the credit base meant that even more loans had to be made available to more people for longer periods of time. After all they had targets to achieve.

By the eighties virtually every area of the economy was dependent on credit. Even consumer items such as food, clothing and travel were dependent on credit through credit cards and small loans. Lenders extended long-term loans based on equity in assets. Thus consumers could borrow on the appreciated value of their homes, stocks and businesses. But since the equity was dependent on the availability of loans to subsequent buyers, this created the need for even more lending. The economy was returning to the pre-Depression mentality of growth through debt.

In the eighties the government was no longer just the guarantor of loans, it was the stimulator of massive debt. The economy had become totally dependent on consumers' borrowing to keep it going. The traditional requirements for qualifying borrowers fell by the wayside as lenders sought wider markets for their loans. No longer was the rule in mortgage loans two times the husband's salary, it was four times both incomes. Car loans were extended to sixty months, and some mortgages were for thirty-five years or more.

By the eighties debt had become the engine that fuelled the entire economy, and consumers were forced to borrow even the equity out of their homes in order to purchase cars and help their children through college. Is it any wonder that in the midst of this steamroller of debt financing the average family experienced financial problems?

It is interesting that the increase in the British divorce rate can be tracked on a curve matching the growth of debt in the country. Does the increase in divorce cause the debt to increase, or is it the other way around? We believe that the increased incidence of divorce is a direct result of too much debt. Over seventy per cent of divorced couples state that financial problems were the primary cause of their divorce.

What can a person do to break out of this cycle? How much credit can an individual or a family handle? These are the fundamental questions that will be addressed in this book. Our intent is twofold. First, we want to help those who are in debt develop a plan to manage their finances. Secondly, we want to convince anyone that he or she can become debt-free and stay that way, given the desire, discipline and time.

We believe that eventually we are heading for a massive economic recession (or depression) during which the present debt cycle will be reversed. Regardless of what anyone says to the contrary, we cannot continue to run our economy on borrowed money. Eventually the debt burden will become so excessive that even the interest payments cannot be made.

Consumers and businesses owe vast amounts in debt, much of it at floating or variable interest rates. Unfortunately, the rates tend to rise when the economy turns sour. Those who are caught in the debt cycle during any major recession quickly discover the meaning of Proverbs 22:7, 'The rich rule over the poor, and the borrower is servant to the lender.' The more you owe means the less control you have of 'your' money. Creditors will be dictating to you what your priorities are. And each month you have to run a little bit faster just to stand still.

CHAPTER 2

SLIDING TOWARDS A CRISIS

Paul and Julie were from middle-class families and grew up in a suburban area of Leeds. Julie's father was a realistic person who kept the household accounts and distributed the money. He gave Julie's mother housekeeping money and he paid all the other bills. He gave Julie a strict allowance and she was expected to work for a portion of her clothing and entertainment money.

In Paul's family the distribution of tasks was different. His mother kept the cheque book and paid the bills. His father never got involved with family finances except when he wanted to buy something. Then he simply wrote a cheque for the amount he needed. That caused some terrible fights since he never bothered to fill in the cheque stubs. Paul could almost always go to his dad and get money when he needed it. When he did this, his father usually told him not to tell his mother because she would have a fit. Paul's father worked a great deal of overtime on his job and believed that the money was his to spend as he wished.

Paul had several part-time jobs while he was growing up, but rarely stayed at any for longer than a few weeks. The money he made was his to spend as he liked. When he was seventeen his father bought him a car and his mother blew up about it because she hadn't been consulted.

When Paul started college he was encouraged to apply for a student loan. He completed two years of college while living at home, but never really decided on a field of study. He took a summer job at a large supermarket and received an offer to stay on permanently, which he accepted.

Paul and Julie went out for nearly a year after they met in college, and when he was offered his permanent job he asked Julie to marry him, with the understanding that she would complete her education in teaching – to which she was very strongly committed.

Neither Paul nor Julie received any detailed instructions from their parents about marriage. It was assumed that the minister of Julie's church would provide the instruction they needed. Indeed, the minister did require several hours of counselling on sex, communication and spiritual values. Once he asked Paul if he would be able to support a family, to which Paul replied, 'Yes, I'm earning £6.50 an hour at the supermarket so we'll have plenty of money.' Since that was more than the minister was making himself (not counting housing or car allowances) he never pursued the subject further. So having completed what they thought were the requirements for marriage, Paul and Julie were married…

Julie read the notice:

> Dear Mr and Mrs Elvers,
> Our records show that your account is seriously overdue. We have made numerous attempts to contact you about this matter. This letter is to notify you that your account has been turned over to our Collections Department. You need to settle this account in total to avoid serious damage to your credit rating.
> Sincerely
> Robert Bowers, Credit Manager

'Oh no, I don't think I can stand much more of this,' Julie thought. 'I work all day long and then come home to this. There doesn't seem to be enough money anymore. I feel like I can never go out and buy myself a new dress, and the nursery said they were going to increase Timothy's fees. I wish I were dead.'

Julie was convinced that she was at the end of her tether emotionally. She resented having to work and felt guilty about leaving her son with strangers every day. She felt trapped.

Meanwhile Paul was trying to cope with feelings of inferiority and with overwhelming financial pressure. Unfortunately, his method of coping tended to amplify Julie's anxieties.

'Hey Paul, we're starting a new company tenpin bowling team. Are you interested in joining?'

'No, I can't. Money's a bit tight at the moment,' Paul replied dejectedly.

'Ah, what's the matter, Paul? Your wife won't let you have enough to go bowling? I told my wife that I do what I want with my money, and if she doesn't like it she can find herself another meal ticket.'

'Maybe that's what Julie is thinking about doing,' Paul thought as he left for the day. 'It seems that all we ever do is argue about money. I feel awful about our row last night, but she acted like it was my fault she has to work. That's so stupid. If she had taken her pills like she was supposed to, she wouldn't have got pregnant and we'd be OK. Women are supposed to know about these things and I can't help it if she can't go to college now.' But Paul knew that his marriage was in serious trouble.

He made his way out to his car with his stomach twisted in knots. He thought about going to a doctor, but he didn't know what to say. He got into his car and turned the key. All he heard in response was a low growl and than a click. 'Oh great,' he said as he looked around the almost empty car park. 'Now what am I going to do?'

Paul got out of his car and went back into the supermarket. He saw one of his colleagues and asked if he would help him jump start his car.

'I'll be glad to,' he replied. 'But you need to do something about that old banger of yours. This is the third time in the last month it wouldn't start.'

'I wish I could do something about it,' Paul thought as they headed out of the door. 'But we seem to get further behind every month. I had a better car when I was in college than I do now.'

In a few minutes they got the car started and Paul was off home. 'Julie's going to be mad again,' Paul said out loud. 'This is the second time I've been late this week.' Then he thought, 'It seems like she's always mad these days. I work as hard as I can and she keeps nagging about how she always has to do without things. I wonder what she thinks I do?'

As Paul was driving by the car showroom he saw a sign that read, 'Why put up with your old car? We'll put you in a new car for only £118 a month. No deposit needed.' He thought, 'I know we can't buy a new car, but it won't hurt to look. I spend more than that on this old pile of junk now, I'll bet.'

An hour later Paul was on his way home, driving a brand-new Ford. He had signed the contracts, but the salesman had assured him that if there was a problem with the car he could trade it back in. Paul was excited to show it to Julie. He knew they could work the £132 a month into their budget somehow. It cost more than the advertised price, but he knew Julie would want a sunroof and one or two little extras.

As he walked through the door he could hear the baby screaming. Julie came out of the kitchen. 'Paul, where have you been? I could use some help around here. Will you please go and see what's the matter with Timothy. I don't think I can stand his crying another minute.' With that she turned back towards the kitchen.

Paul headed into the bedroom to pick up Timothy and snapped, 'I don't know what's wrong with you. You're acting worse than a child.' Julie did an abrupt about-face and followed him into Timothy's room.

'You're a good one to talk,' she yelled, with as much anger as she felt inside. 'I feel like I've got to take care of two children instead of one. The bank sent me a note at work today about our VISA account. If we don't pay it they are going to hand it over to debt collectors. If my boss gets another attachment of earnings order he'll probably sack me.'

'Ah, that's stupid. They can't sack you for that. And the bill's not that much overdue anyway.'

'So I'm stupid now, too, am I?' Julie shouted as she stormed out of the room. 'If I'm that stupid, you probably should have married somebody else.' She slammed the door to their bedroom, and Paul heard the lock click shut.

Depression swept over him as he picked up their son and went into the kitchen. He didn't know where to turn or what to do. 'What would Julie say when she found out about the car?' he wondered. He knew she was seriously considering leaving him again. The last time their minister had been able to talk her into coming back, and the Emergency Fund had helped them catch up on their bills. But he knew that Julie couldn't be talked into coming back if she left him again.

Carrying Timothy with him, Paul went outside and got into the new car. He eased it out of the drive and drove back to the showroom. He hoped he could get his old car back without Julie discovering what he had done. He remembered that the last time she had left was because he had bought a new video recorder.

CHAPTER 3

IT DIDN'T BEGIN YESTERDAY

When Paul and Julie were married he was twenty-two and she was twenty-one. They thought they could handle marriage, but wanted to delay having children for at least five years. That would give Julie time to finish college and get established in her teaching career. Paul thought he would like to go back to college some day, but not until Julie finished.

After living in a flat for five months, Paul decided that it didn't make sense to keep throwing money away on rent. Some of the chaps at work explained that he was losing all the tax concessions the government allowed home owners, so Paul began to look for a home they could buy. He found one that was near their price range, but the bank wouldn't give them a mortgage on his income alone. So during the summer college break Julie took a job as a receptionist for a local dentist. Based on their combined incomes they signed to buy the house. Julie told Paul several times that she didn't think it was a good idea to buy a home, but he assured her that he would be getting salary increases to cover the additional costs. 'Besides,' he said, 'with the tax benefits we'll get, it won't cost us any more than renting.'

They couldn't afford the down payment, so Paul's dad co-signed for a loan. Paul neglected to mention the loan on his mortgage application, and also failed to mention that Julie's income was only temporary. The monthly household bills took almost sixty per cent of Paul's take-home pay. Almost immediately they were in financial trouble from the payments alone. With the insurance, taxes and utilities added, Paul and Julie were on the road to debt without realising it. After the first month Paul was unable to make the loan payment to his bank. When it was sixty days overdue, the bank attached his salary and had the payments deducted automatically as per the agreement. Paul's father was sent written notice of the collection proceedings against him for the two months in arrears. When he received the notice, he hit the roof and stormed over to Paul and Julie's to confront the issue.

Even a casual observer could see at this point that giving Paul and Julie more money was not the answer. But it's often much easier to see the truth in someone else's life than it is in your own. Certainly Paul wasn't trying to deceive anyone. He just didn't have enough information about the way finances worked to make an intelligent decision.

The loan from Julie's father didn't solve any problems. It merely delayed the inevitable. Within two months the bills were mounting up again. Creditors were calling to pressure both Paul and Julie. But most often they wanted to reach Julie because they knew that she would succumb to pressure more easily than her husband.

It was almost impossible for Julie to concentrate on her college work, and for the first time in her life her grades began to slip and that put additional pressure on her. One evening she came home from college, flipped on the light switch and – nothing happened. She made her way to the dining room and tried that switch. Still nothing. She knew their electricity had been cut off.

She found a torch and began to look through the desk in their bedroom where she found two reminders and the warning that their electricity would be cut off if they didn't pay the bill immediately. She also found similar notices from the gas and water companies. She sat there in the dark crying for nearly an hour until Paul came home.

When Paul came in he said, 'Julie, what's the matter with the lights?'

'I'll tell you what's the matter. You haven't paid the bill for the last two months, and they turned our power off. That's what's the matter! And I found notices from the other utilities too. Paul, what's the matter with you? Can't you even keep up with the utility bills?'

'I'm sorry, love. I intended to pay them, but there just wasn't enough money. I'll try and catch up next time I get paid.'

'Oh, Paul, it's always going to be all right next time you get paid. But we never seem to have enough money to catch up. I've decided to leave college and get a job. I just can't live like this anymore.'

'I'm really sorry but I think you're right. If you could just work for a while until we get straight it would really help. You should be able to go back next autumn. I've got another rise coming that will help a lot then.'

Julie finished college and took a job as a typist earning about £700 a month net. She desperately wanted to tithe her income, as she had done all of her unmarried life, but Paul said they couldn't afford to do so. He was supported in that decision by both sets of parents, who felt it would be better to pay off some of the debts first. That turned out to be a spiritual turning point in Julie's life. She had been taught that tithing was a way to keep bad things from happening. When she stopped tithing she expected to have a disaster in her life. When it didn't happen, she began to doubt that there really was a God. If so, why didn't he punish her for not giving her tithe? Shortly after that she stopped attending the church she had gone to all her life. Gradually, but steadily, she began to drift away from her relationship with God.

For several months things seemed to get better financially, and her relationship with Paul improved. They had some extra money to go out periodically, and Julie was able to buy a used car so that she wouldn't be dependent on Paul to get to and from work. Then she began to feel awful in the mornings. When she missed her period she realised that she might be pregnant. She hadn't been disciplined about taking the pill, and a visit to a local health centre confirmed her worst fears: she was pregnant. A general feeling of gloom came over her as she thought about Paul's reaction and the fact that not only would a baby curtail her education, but it would also greatly reduce her ability to work. She felt like she was in a box with no way out. She thought briefly about the prospect of an abortion, but then put it out of her mind. Her strong Christian background would not allow her to do such a thing. But now she understood the terrible temptation that money pressures created for others who found themselves in the same situation.

'What do you mean, you're pregnant?' Paul shouted when Julie told him. 'How could you be so stupid, Julie? All you had to do was take your pills, and you wouldn't have got into this mess.'

'Do you think I got pregnant on purpose?' Julie screamed back. 'I don't like this any more than you do, but there is nothing I can do about it now.'

Paul stormed out of their bedroom. Julie collapsed on the bed in tears. She felt guilty about getting pregnant and anxious about the future. 'How will we ever be able to pay for a baby?' she wondered. 'If I stop working, we won't even be able to pay the bills we have now.'

The rest of that evening Julie stayed in the bedroom and Paul stayed downstairs. He began to feel guilty about his reaction to Julie and decided to apologise. But by the time he went upstairs she was asleep.

Julie continued to work, but morning sickness forced her to miss more and more work. Finally, her boss called her in to confront the issue. 'Julie, I know you've had a tough time with this pregnancy, but you've missed six days in the last two weeks. We need someone to do your work. Why don't you take a month's leave of absence and stay at home? If you're doing better, then come back and see me, and we'll find something for you to do.'

'Oh, Mrs Moore, I can't afford to take time off,' Julie replied through a rush of tears. 'I have to work or we can't keep up with our payments.'

'Julie, I think that you and Paul ought to consider filing for bankruptcy. You're not going to be able to work while you're so sick. And if you continue the way you're going you will ruin your health and the baby's too.'

'Bankruptcy? I never thought about it,' Julie said. 'I thought bankruptcy was only for companies or people who owed millions of pounds.'

'No, dear,' Mrs Moore replied. 'My husband's firm handles personal bankruptcies all the time. It's certainly no sin to file for bankruptcy any more. After all, those companies that lend to young couples ought to know better anyway. Here's one of my husband's cards. Talk things over with Paul and give him a ring if you would like to talk about it.'

That evening Julie was quiet and Paul sensed that something new was wrong, but he dreaded asking what it was. Their relationship had been so tense since Julie became pregnant that they rarely spoke to one another without getting into some kind of argument. Finally, he spoke up. 'What's wrong now, Julie? You have barely said two words since we got home.'

'I lost my job today,' she replied matter-of-factly.

'You lost your job!' Paul bellowed as he came up out of the chair. 'How did you lose your job?'

'Mrs Moore said I was taking too much time off, and they needed someone who is more consistent.'

'They can't do that. It's illegal,' Paul shouted in fear, as much as anger.

'Yes they can, Paul,' Julie replied. 'They're willing to give me another job when I can work again. But Mrs Moore is right. If I keep up this pace, it may be detrimental to the baby's health.'

'But what in the world will we do?' Paul said in despair as he sat down again. 'We've just bought your car and we can barely survive even when you're working.'

'Mrs Moore suggested that we file for bankruptcy,' Julie replied. 'She said her husband handles bankruptcies for couples like us all the time.'

'I don't see how that's possible,' Paul replied. 'Most of our debts are credit cards and store cards, apart from the house and cars. I don't think you can get out of those debts.'

'She said we can,' Julie replied, handing Paul the business card Mrs Moore had given her.

Paul arranged a meeting with the insolvency practitioner, Joe Moore. 'I've looked at your case, and I think I can help you,' he said. 'Most of your debts are relatively small bills owed to credit card companies and stores. And since you're really in this mess because of an unplanned pregnancy, your creditors may accept an IVA proposal.'

'What is an IVA?' Paul asked.

'It's an individual voluntary arrangement, set up for cases just like yours where a couple gets into debt over their heads through hardship. You can offer a regular monthly payment to your creditors out of your income. You probably won't be able to pay the whole of what you owe, but you can ask the creditors to accept it in full and final settlement of your debts.'

'And that's all there is to it?' Paul said in amazement. 'A regular monthly payment – and we don't have to pay all our debts?'

'That's about it,' Mr Moore replied. 'I've seen it help dozens of couples just like you. After all, it's not your fault that Julie can't work anymore. And the letter you received from her company telling her to stay at home for at least a month will really help sell this to the court.'

'I don't feel completely at peace about this,' Julie said. 'What about the rest of the money we owe? Isn't it our responsibility to pay all of it?'

'Absolutely not. In the first place the creditors carry bad debt insurance to protect them against losses. And secondly, this law is to protect young couples like you from abuse by ruthless collection agencies that try to get blood out of a stone.'

'We certainly have been harassed by collection agencies,' Julie said to herself. 'Well I suppose if the law allows it, there is no problem. What do you think, Paul?'

'I think it's an answer to prayer, I don't know what we would have done with you losing your job and a baby on the way. Mr Moore, please go ahead with the IVA.'

'There's just one more thing. My fee for setting up the IVA will be two thousand pounds.'

'Two thousand pounds,' said Paul in surprise. 'We don't have two thousand pounds.'

'Could you get it from your parents?' he asked.

'We have already borrowed from our parents,' said Julie. 'I don't think any of them would agree to lend us any more.'

'That's too bad,' said Mr Moore. 'I need the money up front before I can take the case, but there is another alternative.'

'What's that?' asked Paul.

'Why don't you put your groceries and utilities on your credit cards for the next month? Then you'll have the money you need. When the IVA takes effect the charges will be lumped in with the other bills.'

'But is that honest?' asked Julie.

'Of course,' replied Mr Moore. 'Besides, why do you think the credit card companies charge so much interest? They can afford to take a few losses. They're not hurting financially. If you don't believe that, just have a look at their offices sometime.'

'That's true,' agreed Paul. 'Besides, I don't see that we have any alternative. This seems like an answer to our prayers. Now you'll be able to stay at home until the baby's born. By then I'll be getting overtime pay again, and you'll be able to go back to college.'

'Sound's good,' Mr Moore replied. 'Remember, when the bills come in next month just put them aside until after the creditor's meeting. Just pay what you have to in order to keep the lights on. But don't put the cash in your bank account or it will become part of your assets. Just keep it in your home somewhere safe.'

'Thanks for your help,' Paul said as they got up to leave.

After they left Julie said, 'Paul, I don't like the idea of using our credit cards when we know we're not going to pay the bills.'

'Listen, Julie, Mr Moore seemed like a nice chap and I trust him. I'm sure he wouldn't tell us to do something illegal. Besides, what alternative do we have? With you pregnant we can't pay any of the bills anyway. And as Mr Moore said, the companies can afford the loss. That's why they carry insurance.'

CHAPTER 4

THINGS COME TO A HEAD

'Mr and Mrs Elvers, my credit card company clients are prepared to vote to approve your proposal for an IVA. You need to understand that each month you must meet the minimum payments agreed with your creditors. Failure to do so will constitute a default in IVA and may require your Supervisor, Mr Brown, to instigate bankruptcy proceedings. Do you understand?'

'Yes, we do,' replied Paul.

'There is one further matter which concerns my clients. There were several charges on your credit cards during the last month prior to this meeting of creditors. My clients have requested that these items be excluded from the IVA on the grounds that they were made in contemplation of the forthcoming IVA meeting. My clients will require an amendment to the IVA requiring you to pay them separately. I want to issue you both a stern warning that my clients could in fact initiate a prosecution for fraud, but on the condition that you pay these sums separately they are prepared to give another opportunity to you in the light of your special circumstances.

'I want to issue you both a stern warning that this court will not condone or allow such blatant attempts to deceive your creditors. The bankruptcy court is provided to give couples who have had personal financial setbacks beyond their control the chance to start over again. It is not to be used to defraud those who trusted you by extending credit to you.

'I hope you have learned from your bad experiences with the overuse of credit and that you will not repeat the same mistakes. You're young and can re-establish your lives and your credit if you discipline yourselves. The next time, the creditors are less likely to deal with you so leniently.'

Julie sat in stunned silence. She didn't really hear what the creditor's representative said beyond the point where he chastened them for what he concluded to be an attempt to defraud the credit card companies. She realised that that was exactly what they had attempted to do.

'What's the matter, Julie?' Paul asked.

'Oh, Paul, I'm so ashamed of what we tried to do by putting all our expenses on our credit cards and hoarding our money. Those men from the credit card companies must think we're awful people.'

'Don't worry about it, Julie,' Joe Moore said. 'Our plan worked, and now your total debt payments will be just two hundred pounds a month. And with the creditors agreeing to a thirty per cent payback you should be clear in four years.'

'I don't understand what that means,' Paul said.

'It means that you must repay the existing debts up to thirty per cent of their current levels, but with no interest running.'

'You mean we don't have to repay the entire amount?' Paul asked in astonishment.

'No, the creditors agreed that it would be an undue burden on you to repay the entire amount.'

'But I think we should repay the entire amount,' Julie said. 'After all, we did borrow the money in good faith. I don't think it would be right to repay less.'

'I appreciate your attitude, Julie, but you need to be realistic. You have a baby on the way and you'll have additional expenses. Don't you think your first responsibility is to your baby?'

'Yes,' Julie replied. 'But…'

'I agree with Mr Moore,' replied Paul. 'I think this is an answer from God.'

'Of course,' responded Joe Moore. 'Even God provided a way to set aside debts so that his people wouldn't be caught up in debts they couldn't repay.'

'He did?' Julie said in amazement.

'Absolutely. In the Old Testament God had a plan where every seven years all debts would be set aside. That's where our bankruptcy laws originated.'

'I never heard anybody explain that before,' Paul said. 'So God allows bankruptcy.'

'Of course,' replied Joe Moore. 'Otherwise I wouldn't be in this business.'

'What's going to happen to the credit card bills we ran up last month?' Paul asked.

'The repayment plan will include those debts each month, but you'll have to repay one hundred per cent of what's owed on them. It just means it will take a little longer to get out of debt, but it's no big deal. That's always a risk you run when you charge expenses to your account just before a bankruptcy hearing. But I knew the judge wouldn't throw your case out – not with Julie pregnant.'

'You mean you knew the creditors might not allow the recent charges to be set aside, Mr Moore?' said Julie in astonishment.

'Well, I knew it was a possibility. But in this business, nothing ventured, nothing gained. Besides, you're no worse off than you might have otherwise been.'

'Except for our reputation,' replied Julie as tears welled up in her eyes.

As they were going home Julie commented, 'Paul, I don't think we did the right thing. I think we have cheated our creditors.'

'I disagree,' said Paul. 'It feels like a burden has been lifted off our shoulders. We have a chance to start afresh and get our lives back in order. Wait and see; things are going to work out OK from now on.'

As the weeks passed, Julie began to believe that Paul was right. The pressures on their marriage eased as the financial strain from outstanding bills lessened. For several weeks Paul was able to work extra overtime and they used the extra money to buy things for the baby. Julie was even able to return to work on a part-time basis, so they had more 'free' money than at any time previously in their marriage.

The baby came, and Julie was totally occupied with learning to care for him. Her mother helped until the baby was nearly a month old, and then left to return to her own home. During the fifth week the baby began to cry more than usual and Julie took him for a general check-up. The doctor diagnosed colic. As the weeks passed the baby cried more frequently, and eventually it seemed as though he cried nearly every waking moment. Both Julie's and Paul's nerves began to wear thin.

Paul began to get lax about paying the household bills and he began to pick up food in the evenings rather than cook at home. The baby took up so much of Julie's time that she was virtually unable to do anything else.

One evening, on the way home from work, Paul was involved in a minor car accident. He was required to appear in court the following month. He didn't mention the incident to Julie and reckoned he could scrape together the money to pay the fine, which he thought would be about £35. Paul put the incident out of his mind and completely forgot about the court date. Late one evening, after arriving home from work, he answered the doorbell to find two policemen at his front door.

'Are you Paul Elvers?' the older policeman asked.

'Yes,' Paul answered. 'What can I do for you?'

'Mr Elvers, I have a warrant for your arrest for failure to appear in court to answer charges on a traffic offence and for driving a vehicle without insurance,' the officer said.

'Oh no!' Paul exclaimed. 'I completely forgot about the

ticket. But there must be some mistake. I do have insurance on my car.'

'Sir, I would suggest that you get a copy of your policy and come with us. We have a warrant for your arrest and you'll either have to pay the fines or post bail to be released.'

'How much are the fines?' Paul asked as Julie came to the door to see what was going on.

'The total is £350.'

'There must be some mistake,' Paul exclaimed. They can't be as much as £350.'

'Yes sir, they are,' replied the officer. 'They include a traffic offence, a fine for failure to have insurance and the court summons charges.'

'I know I have insurance,' Paul said defiantly. 'Wait here, and I'll get the documents.'

Julie began to feel a familiar wave of depression come over her as she heard the conversation. She suspected that the officer was right and Paul was wrong. Her suspicions were confirmed when Paul returned a few minutes later.

'I found the policy but it has lapsed. I'm afraid that I forgot to pay the premium. It must have been cancelled without their telling me.'

'You mean my husband will have to spend the night in a cell?' she asked, almost in panic.

'Yes, madam,' the officer replied.

With that they led Paul out to the police car and placed him in the back seat. Julie rushed to the phone and called her father to tell him what had happened. 'Calm down, darling,' her father said. 'It'll be OK. We'll go down first thing in the morning and get Paul out. In the meantime, why don't you come over here and spend the night with us?' Julie willingly agreed. Her fear and depression were rising to a peak as she thought about the whole cycle of debt and money pressures starting all over again.

The next morning Julie's father put up the money for the bail and Paul was released. On the way home Julie questioned him about their finances and Paul confessed that several bills were outstanding.

'There just doesn't seem to be enough money each month,' Paul said. 'There was for a while, but it seems to evaporate. We just can't manage on my salary, Julie. You're going to have to go to work.'

'But, Paul, we don't have anyone to look after the baby,' Julie said as the tears began to flow. She felt like she was in a dark pit and the sides were beginning to cave in.

'Maybe your mum would look after him, at least for a while, until we can catch up with some of the bills,' said Paul.

'I hate doing that,' Julie screamed. 'We're always asking someone to bail us out of our messes. I wish I had never met you, Paul.'

Julie did go back to work and found that she actually enjoyed it. The baby was getting better, and being away from him during the day helped her to cope with the evenings. But soon her mother told her that she couldn't look after him any longer. She had a life of her own to lead, and it wasn't fair that she was being expected to bring up a second family. Julie cried a lot over the decision, but in the end she knew her mother was right, so she started looking for someone else to look after her baby. She was shocked at the cost of child care, but eventually she selected what she thought would be the best nursery even though it was going to cost around £350 a month.

As the weeks passed, she and Paul continued to argue about money. Julie believed she was a slave to Paul's impulses. He often bought things he wanted – such as a new television or a CD player – but then there was no money for clothes or eating out. Finally, she decided that she would keep a portion of her salary for herself. Instead of taking the cheque home as she had always done in the past, she would stop off at the bank and deposit it, taking out the money she needed.

Paul was furious when she told him about it. 'Julie, you can't do that,' he shouted. 'There won't be enough money to pay the bills.'

'Then they will have to go unpaid,' Julie yelled back. 'I'm not going to worry about it anymore. You never paid my dad back for your fines, and I'm going to start paying him back something every month. Paul, you're a totally irresponsible little boy. I'm sick and tired of working all day and never being able to spend any of my own money.'

'Well, if it's your money, why don't you just keep it yourself, and I'll keep my money!' Paul shouted as he stormed out of the room.

'Then I'll do just that,' Julie yelled back as he slammed the front door.

Julie spent the next two hours drawing up a budget dividing their respective expenses. She decided that she should pay for the baby's nursery costs, her transport, and a fourth of the utilities.

The next day she left work a little early so that she could go to the bank and open an account in her name. That evening she informed Paul that she had decided to keep her money and pay her own bills. She handed him a copy of the division of expenses she had drawn up. Paul had a sinking feeling inside, as if something had died. And in truth he knew that something had: their marriage.

'Look Julie, I'm sorry for what I said last night. I didn't mean it really. I don't want us to have separate bank accounts and split the expenses.'

'No, you just want to be able to spend what you want, when you want,' Julie spat out. 'Well, no more. You pay your part and I'll pay my part from now on. And if you don't like it, I'll leave.'

'Do you really mean that?' Paul asked with a hurt look on his face.

'I really do,' she replied defiantly. 'I don't know if I love you anymore, but I do know that I don't respect you. I've been on the giving end of our marriage from the first day. From now on I'm going to do what's best for me.'

Paul felt as if someone had just hit him in the stomach with a sledgehammer. 'Where did we go wrong?' Paul thought as Julie stormed out of the dining room. 'How could I have been so stupid as to let our relationship slip into hatred? I don't know what to do now.' For the first time in a long time Paul fell to his knees and asked God to forgive him and help him to heal his marriage.

CHAPTER 5

IF ONLY THE BABY
HAD BEEN WELL

Paul and Julie Elvers are not unique. Perhaps the exact circumstances are different in the lives of other couples, but the end result is the same in millions of marriages throughout Britain. Like Paul and Julie, most couples start out with the highest expectations for their marriages. Nearly half end in divorce – the majority of those because of financial problems. Unfortunately, few young couples know what they did to create their financial problems or what they need to do to solve them. But before discussing how to solve financial problems, here is the story of another couple.

John and Mary Thompson were both graduates of Bible college. When they left college they both got a job at the same Christian school in the south of England. While they were working there they fell in love and got married. They both came from Christian homes but were from very different economic backgrounds. Mary's father was a successful dentist and although he was not wealthy by any means, he made a very comfortable living. Mary was not indulged as a child and she was expected to work to help pay her way from her teenage years on. While she was at college she was expected to work during the summer to earn money for books, clothes and incidentals, which she did.

John came from a much more modest background. His

mother and father were divorced when he was nine years old. His mother struggled financially after the divorce and money was always in short supply in his home. He got support from his church to attend Bible college, but he had to work long hours to pay his expenses while he was there.

John and Mary had been married for two years when they had their first child. The school they worked for paid low salaries and they had been unable to accumulate any significant savings. But they thought they would be able to manage financially if they were careful. The baby would be born during the summer holidays, so Mary would be able to work almost up to the time of the birth.

There were two things they hadn't planned on. One was that regardless of how much they scrimped and saved, John's salary alone was too low to meet their minimum needs. And two, that the baby would have major health problems. He was born with brain damage and other major complications and required constant attention. Mary was unable to return to work.

Within six months of the baby's birth they had debts of almost £6,000 and were sinking further behind every month. When they attempted to pay the mortgage arrears, they fell behind on payments for their monthly living expenses. If they tried to keep up on their living expenses, they fell further behind with the mortgage. By the seventh month some of their debts had been turned over to collection agencies and Mary was getting frequent, sometimes abusive, calls at home. She was an emotional wreck, and her paediatrician – who was a friend from church – suggested that John consider making himself bankrupt to relieve the financial pressure.

Coming home from the hospital Mary asked, 'What do you think about what Doctor Reese said?'

'I don't know. I've always believed that you should pay your bills, but that seems to be impossible in our case. Every month we get further behind with the bills. What do you think?'

'I don't know the answer, either. But I do know I can't live under the kind of pressure I feel right now. We can't pay the bills anyway, so I don't see what difference it would make if I make myself bankrupt. If we're ever able to pay, we can always start repaying the bills, can't we?'

'I suppose so,' Jack replied. 'I don't feel at peace about it, but I honestly don't know of another alternative. I'll call Bill Johnson a solicitor I know and ask if he handles this sort of thing. But as it stands, we don't even have the money it takes to go bankrupt.'

CHAPTER 6

THREE PERSONAL TRAITS
THAT LEAD TO DEBT

How did Paul and Julie, and John and Mary, get into debt? They did so because of three things: ignorance, indulgence and poor planning.

Ignorance

Paul and Julie represent the majority of young couples today, Christian and non-Christian alike. They enter marriage with little or no understanding of finances and quickly find themselves overwhelmed by the opportunities they encounter to spend more than they make. Since opposites do attract, usually one partner is an optimist, who generally looks towards the future to straighten out any errors in the present. The other is a worrier, who needs stability and security. The optimists don't purposely lie to their spouse, but convince themselves that things will change for the better. Paul was an optimist.

Julie, the worrier, became suspicious of Paul because of what appeared to be deceptions and financial irresponsibility. She was forced to drop out of college and give up her career plans, for which she blamed Paul. The additional pressure of an unplanned baby added to their financial problems, plus the fact that he was a screaming, colicky child. So Julie developed great hostility.

After counselling a multitude of young and old couples in circumstances nearly identical to Paul and Julie's, we can say with some degree of certainty that the financial situation in which they found themselves was indicative of their lack of financial education and knowledge. They were not stupid – just ignorant. As Proverbs 22:3 says, 'A prudent man sees danger and takes refuge, but the simple keep going and suffer for it.'

Julie's reaction could be the subject for an entire book. It was fed by unrealistic and unbiblical desires for self-fulfilment. Apparently she had been taught that her worth as a woman was dependent on attaining a degree and developing a career outside the home. Neither of those goals is bad in itself, except where they conflict with God's greater plan for someone – in this case that of wife and mother.

Paul, on the other hand, was living in a dream world of his own and angering his wife as he did so. He refused to take responsibility for his decisions and tried to blame their problem on Julie. If she went to work, their problems would be solved. If she had taken her pill she wouldn't have got pregnant. God directed the husband to protect and comfort his wife, but Paul tried to shift the blame to her and sneak around behind her back with his personal indulgences.

Indulgence

Indulgence, impulse buying, and get-rich-quick schemes all have the same root cause: greed. Most of us don't like to hear that because we're all prone to at least one of these problems. In reality, they are just different levels of the same basic problem. Some people might indulge themselves through buying shares, just as others might through the purchase of expensive cars, houses or clothes. Each of us has special indulgences that stem from an attitude of lust. Lust is not limited to the area of sex. In our society more people may lust after power and wealth than after sex.

Often we have the mistaken idea that more money will solve our financial problems. More money can easily result in bigger problems. Men who invest in high-risk deals that fail often transfer the blame to other people. Since the family is the most readily available scapegoat, they are the ones who usually receive the blame. 'I was doing it so that I could make better provision for my family,' the man says. Nonsense. He did it because it fed his ego and was a chance to get rich quickly.

Poor planning

At first glance, it appears that John and Mary fell into financial difficulty through no fault of their own. And that is true to some extent. Who could have predicted the problems they had with their first child? Only God could have done so. But their break-even point was beyond John's income. Without Mary working they simply couldn't manage.

The symptom they faced was debt, but the real problem was poor planning. They had never been trained in finances and did not know how to establish a budget. John took a teaching position that did not have the potential to meet the most basic needs of his family, at least without Mary's income. So the difficulties they faced because of the baby did not cause their financial problems – they merely amplified them.

CHAPTER 7

THE BIBLE SPEAKS ON DEBT AND BORROWING

We have seen how two different couples got into debt. Now we need to examine how they got out of debt, because ultimately they did. Their marriages survived because the couples were willing to work together and do the things required to put their financial affairs in order, no matter how difficult.

But before we do that, we need to discuss the principles the Bible gives concerning debt and borrowing, for much of the advice on debt in this book is based on those principles.

Biblical principles

1. The debtor is in servitude to the one who lends to him

Debt is not a well-understood term today. Most people use the word *debt* to describe any borrowing but, although that is not entirely inaccurate, it is not precise enough. Scripture goes beyond that definition to describe the conditions of indebtedness. Even if a debt is current (all payments up to date) the borrower is potentially in a position of servitude according to Proverbs 22:7, 'The rich rule over the poor, and the borrower is servant to the lender.' But if the debt is outstanding the lender is given an implied authority from God, according to the Bible. In the time of Christ that authority extended to imprisonment, slavery and the confiscation of a borrower's total worldly possessions. Not once in the Bible is there even a hint that that was not the legitimate right of a lender. The only variable Scripture allows is that if the lender and the borrower were both Jews, the borrower would be released from servitude at the end of seven years, unless he voluntarily elected to remain a slave. To say the least, borrowing was not a decision to be taken lightly.

The same basic rules applied in Britain, even in the twentieth century, as the records from debtors' prisons will show. It is evident that our attitudes today regarding debt vary somewhat from our predecessors. The cause of this difference can be pinpointed as greed and indulgence. Not on the part of the borrowers, that came later. The initial greed was on the part of the government, which saw debt as a way of expanding the economy. This required a drastic alteration of the rules regarding borrowing and the consequences of failure to pay.

Few people today are willing to risk forfeiting their freedom and separation from their families to borrow money. The risk would simply be too great. So the laws were amended to make borrowing less risky and credit more available. And besides, who would tolerate the government borrowing massive amounts of money that could not be repaid while friends and relatives languished in prison for failure to repay their personal loans?

The old laws for outstanding debts seem harsh and unnecessarily cruel to us today. (However, even today there are more people in prison for non-payment of fines than for any other reason.) But the principles behind them were sound and just. The laws assumed that nobody was forced to borrow money – that people borrowed money voluntarily. The lender extended money and the borrower represented himself as trustworthy. The punishment for defaulting on a debt was actually more severe than for theft because it was considered a breach of trust.

2. Borrowing is permitted in Scripture

Some well-intentioned teachers have taken the position that all borrowing is prohibited according to God's word and that, consequently, Christians should not be involved in any borrowing or lending. Almost without exception the biblical reference that such teachers use to support their position is Romans 13:8, 'Let no debt remain outstanding, except the continuing debt to love one another, for he who loves his fellow-man has fulfilled the law.'

If only it were that simple. When you first look at Romans 13:8 it does seem as if it provides justification for telling Christians to get rid of credit, especially those who have misused it. But if God intended to tell his people that *all* borrowing was prohibited, why are there so many New Testament verses instructing people to repay what they borrow?

Of course, God may have decided that it was time for his people to become totally debt-free, and thus in the New Testament changed the rules that had previously held true concerning indebtedness. But only those two alternatives exist: either God changed the rules for his people and we had better start the business of eliminating debt immediately, or Romans 13:8 does not mean that Christians should never borrow anything.

To understand Romans 13:8 it is necessary to go back to Romans 13:6 where Paul discusses the payment of taxes. Christians in Paul's day often took the position that they should not have to pay taxes to the government of Rome because it was a heathen government. Paul admonished the believers that as Roman subjects they were to obey the laws regarding taxes. When he did this he was keeping in mind the Lord's discussion of taxes in Matthew 22:17-21 and that he believed that it was unscriptural for Christians to refuse to pay their taxes. In Romans 13:7 Paul expanded and restated his instructions concerning the payment of taxes: 'Give everyone what you owe him: If you owe taxes, pay taxes; if revenue, then revenue; if respect, then respect; if honour, then honour.'

With the background of verses 6 and 7 in mind, Paul's directive to Christians to 'owe no man' anything takes on a different significance than it might if it were read in isolation. Paul was summing up the legally-prescribed duty that all men had to pay their taxes and respect government officials. He was not giving a new teaching on the subject of borrowing money, but rather was reiterating a previous admonition to obey the law. Thus we can say that although borrowing is not promoted scripturally, it is not prohibited either.

Principles of borrowing appear in God's word, although it needs to be remembered that these are principles, not laws. From time to time an overzealous teacher will present principles as if they were laws. They are not. A *principle* is an instruction from the Lord to help guide our decision. A *law* is an absolute. Negative consequences may follow from ignoring a principle, but punishment is the likely consequence of ignoring a law God has given us.

An example from our society is drinking and driving. A good rule, or principle, to follow is never to drink too much, but the law says if you drink too much and drive, you will lose your licence and perhaps go to prison.

The principle of borrowing given in Scripture is that it is better not to go surety on a loan. 'A man lacking in judgment strikes hands in pledge and puts up security for his neighbour' (Prov 17:18). Surety means that you have taken on an obligation to pay someone else's debt if they don't.

The law of borrowing given in Scripture is that it is a sin to borrow and not repay. 'The wicked borrow and do not repay, but the righteous give generously' (Psalm 37:21). The assumption in the verse is that the wicked person can repay but will not, as opposed to the individual who wants to repay but cannot.

Principles are given to keep us clearly within God's path so that we can experience his blessings. To ignore them puts us in a constant state of jeopardy in which Satan can cause us to stumble at any time.

3. Debt is not normal

Regardless of how it may seem today, debt is not normal in any economy and should not be normal for God's people. We live in a debt-ridden society that is now virtually dependent on a constant expansion of credit to keep the economy going. That is a symptom of a society no longer willing to follow God's directions. We see this disobedience in various issues such as abortion, pornography and adultery. And yet Christians who wouldn't think of actively participating in these other areas, naively follow the world's path in the area of credit.

Listen to the promise God made to his people: 'If you fully obey the LORD your God and carefully follow all his commands that I give you today, the LORD your God will set you high above all the nations on earth... The LORD will open the heavens, the storehouse of his bounty, to send rain on your land in season and to bless all the work of your hands. *You will lend to many nations but you will borrow from none*' (Deut 28:1,12; emphasis added).

4. Do not accumulate long-term debt

It's hard to believe that a typical British family accepts a twenty-five year mortgage as normal today, or that it is now possible to borrow on a home for nearly thirty-five years. The need to expand the borrowing base continually forces longer mortgage loans. Why? Because expansion through taking on debt causes prices to rise through inflation. As prices rise, mortgages lengthen.

Inflation is a reflection of the expansion of the money supply via borrowed money. For example, the average home in Britain sells for nearly £70,000. Since the average income in Britain is only about £16,000, those two averages just don't add up. Today it requires nearly fifty per cent of the average family's net income to buy the average home (with its attendant charges) even with a twenty-five year mortgage. But what is that average home really worth? To determine that, assume that homes could no longer be sold using long-term mortgages. How much would the average home sell for if it could be bought with cash only? Certainly not for £70,000. It would probably begin to sell at between £10,000 and £15,000. All of the additional cost is inflation created through the use of long-term debt.

The longest term of debt God's people took on in the Bible was about seven years. During the year of remission (the seventh year) the Jew was instructed to release his brother from any indebtedness. 'At the end of every seven years you must cancel debts. This is how it is to be done: Every creditor shall cancel the loan he has made to his fellow Israelite. He shall not require payment from his fellow Israelite or brother, because the LORD's time for cancelling debts has been proclaimed' (Deut 15:1-2). Thus the only debts that could exceed seven years were those made to non-Jews or from non-Jews.

5. Avoid surety

By now you understand that surety means accepting an obligation to pay someone else's debt without having a certain way to make that payment. The most recognisable form of surety is co-signing for the loan of another. But surety can also be any form of borrowing in which you sign an unconditional guarantee to pay.

The only way to avoid surety is to secure a loan against property that will cover the indebtedness, no matter what. Many home buyers think that because they buy an appreciating asset such as a home, they are safe from surety, but that is not so. For example, a lender can sue to collect a deficit on a home mortgage in the event of a default. And remember that most defaults happen during a bad economic cycle, when prices of homes are most likely to drop.

Credit card purchases have become the most common form of surety in our generation. In this transaction one merchant sells you the material and another finances the purchase (except for some in-store cards). In the event of a default, the return of the merchandise does not cancel the debt because the finance company has no interest in the merchandise.

6. The borrower has an absolute commitment to repay

In this generation situation ethics (doing what is best for you in your current situation immediately) is widely accepted, so it is easy to rationalise not paying a debt, especially when one's financial situation seems to be out of control, as with John and Mary. Both the divorce rate and the number of bankruptcies in Britain attest to the fact that we are a situational society. The media present unrealistic expectations of what a marriage should be like, and the 'me' generation expects individual rights to be totally upheld in a marriage. When those unrealistic expectations fail to materialise, nearly half of all spouses call it a day.

The same can be said of those who borrow money. The easy access to credit today leads many people to believe that paying their debts will be a doddle. Unfortunately, many borrowers discover that it is possible for them to accumulate far more debt than they can repay and still maintain the lifestyle they want. As a result, they bail out. Many hundreds, or even thousands, every year in Britain choose bankruptcy as a way to avoid repayment. Yet the average indebtedness for couples who go bankrupt is not a massive sum.

Some Christian teachers draw a parallel between modern law on bankruptcy and the year of jubilee prescribed by God in Leviticus 25:10, 'Consecrate the fiftieth year and proclaim liberty throughout the land to all its inhabitants. It shall be a jubilee for you; each one of you is to return to his family property and each to his own clan.'

There is a view that the year of jubilee and voluntary bankruptcy are comparable, but they aren't. Voluntary bankruptcy can be an act by a borrower to avoid his or her creditors. The year of jubilee (as well as the year of remission) was a voluntary act by a lender to forgive indebtedness – a significant difference.

In some situations a voluntary bankruptcy is acceptable, but only in the context of trying to protect the creditors, or because of extreme emotional and/or family pressures – never in the context of trying to avoid repayment. A Christian needs to accept the hard truth that God allows him no alternative but to keep his promises. That is why the Bible warns him often to be careful before making vows. 'It is better not to vow than to make a vow and not fulfil it' (Eccles 5:5).

CHAPTER 8

LEARN TO FACE REALITY

How did Paul and Julie Elvers get themselves out of debt? It took hard work and a commitment to follow scriptural principles concerning the handling of money.

Paul realised that he had placed his marriage in jeopardy and that Julie was poised to leave at any time. She had left twice before over disputes concerning money, but had returned when Paul promised he would not repeat his mistakes. It was entirely likely that Julie would not return if she were to leave a third time.

Several times in the past Julie had asked Paul to call her minister and make an appointment for counselling. Paul had always refused, saying that he knew more about handling money than the average minister. And he always promised that there would be more income just around the corner that would solve their problems. But after Julie opened her own bank account, it was Paul who asked her if she would go to see the minister with him. She flatly refused. 'No minister is going to be able to help our marriage,' she thought. 'It's finished.'

As she was driving to work that morning it struck her: her marriage really was finished. 'But why? Do I still love Paul?' she wondered. 'I don't know. Our whole married life has been one continual struggle with money.' All day she thought about her options and silently prayed. As far as she was concerned, her marriage was finished – and she didn't know what she was going to do. She had purposely opened her own bank account so that she could accumulate some funds if, and when, she decided to leave. But she knew she didn't make enough money to pay for child care, a house, a car and other expenses. She was shocked by her own thoughts. She had actually been planning to leave Paul. Then she realised that it was not a divorce she wanted. She wanted to be free of the pressures they had been facing since the day they got married. Paul was a good man and she believed he loved her. It was just that he was so irresponsible with money.

That evening Julie found Paul already at home and preparing dinner in the kitchen. 'Paul,' she said in genuine astonishment, 'why are you home so early? Is anything wrong at work?'

'No,' Paul said without looking up. 'I've just realised that because of my stupidity I have lost something very precious to me. Julie, it's not more money I need. I need help. I called Pastor Hurley today and explained what a mess I've made of our finances and our marriage. He is willing to work with me on the marriage, but he recommended a debt counsellor in the church, Mr Woods, who would be willing to help with our finances.'

'Paul, I think that's great,' Julie said with enthusiasm.

'But the debt counsellor won't meet unless we both go. I didn't know what to tell him,' Paul said with tears in his eyes.

'Call him and tell him we'll both be there,' Julie said as she gave Paul a big hug. 'I just pray there is a way out of the mess we're in.'

The next day Paul and Julie went to the debt counsellor. Before he met them he asked them each to complete a short personality test. A few minutes later he called them both into his office. 'Come in,' he said in a friendly tone. 'Take a seat, and let's begin with prayer.'

As Mr Woods was asking the Lord to give them wisdom in

their time together, Paul realised that it had been months since he had even felt the desire to pray or read the Bible, although both had been his habit for most of his life. The pressures they were under seemed to have stripped him of his ability to concentrate. He realised that the same must have been true for Julie, only more so.

When he finished praying, Mr Woods said, 'Paul, tell me what you think the problems are.'

Paul was taken aback by the question. He had expected Mr Woods to ask to see the multitude of records they had brought with them. 'I honestly don't know,' Paul answered. 'I suppose it has to be my handling of the money. We never seem to have enough to pay all the bills. We still owe Julie's dad for most of the loan he made to reinstate our car insurance. We owe for two cars, a consolidation loan with the bank, and our house.'

'Thanks, Paul,' Mr Woods said. 'Julie, what do you think the problem is?'

'Well, I suppose it's much like Paul said, except that I believe the real problem – at least in our marriage – is that we don't discuss things. We argue, and I see it getting worse instead of better.'

'Are you willing to make the changes necessary to cure the problems, rather than just treat the symptoms?' Mr Woods asked.

'I'm ready to do whatever I have to do.' Paul said.

'I think I am, too,' Julie agreed. 'But is this going to be one of those lectures about wives obeying their husbands and being silent in the home?'

'I certainly don't think so,' replied Mr Woods. 'Especially since I believe God put you two together to operate as a team. I generally find that the wife brings a needed perspective to the finances. But the specific problems must be dealt with first. Then we'll decide who should do what. I need to get an idea about where you are financially right now. So I'm going to ask you some questions.'

With that, Mr Woods took out one of his budget work

sheets and started working through the list of monthly expenses. Paul gave most of the answers, but when it came to regular expenses, such as clothes, food, and child care he deferred to Julie's better memory. When they had completed the list, Mr Woods began to list their outstanding debts. Paul was noticeably hesitant once they had gone through the obvious debts, such as the mortgage, bank loan, car loans and family loans.

'What's the problem, Paul?' Mr Woods asked, sensing that Paul was holding something back.

'I need to tell you something,' Paul said hesitantly. 'But I'm afraid Julie will get really upset if I do.'

'I can't help unless I know all the facts,' Mr Woods said. 'If you owe something else that's not shown in our records, you need to let me know about it.'

'Well, about six months ago when Julie and I were having a lot of problems, I bought a new car,' Paul confessed.

'You bought a new car!' Julie exclaimed. 'How did you buy a new car? I've never seen it.'

'Julie, give Paul a chance to explain,' Mr Woods said. 'He is trying to be honest with you now.'

'I bought the car from a local dealer with the understanding that I could return it if Julie wanted me to. When I got home we had a big argument about the electricity being cut off, and Julie left for a couple of days. In the meantime I tried to return the car and found that the dealer wanted six hundred and fifty pounds to take it back.'

'Paul, how could you do that without even asking me?' Julie said with anger in her voice.

'Wait a minute, Julie. Let Paul explain. What's done is done. Let's try to work this out,' Mr Woods said calmly.

'Julie, I know it was stupid and I should have asked you, but I just got carried away when I stopped to look at the cars. And I honestly thought I could return it. I didn't know they would charge a fee for returning it.'

'Where does the car loan stand now, Paul?' Mr Woods asked.

'I signed a note for £650 so they would take the car back. Now they're threatening to sue me if I don't pay up. But I don't know where the money will come from.'

'OK, a £650 bill due now,' Mr Woods noted on his sheet. 'Anything else?'

'One thing,' Paul replied as he looked at Julie and saw her grimace. 'I owe £500 on our VISA for a car stereo I bought a couple of months ago.'

'I thought you saved the money to buy that stereo from your overtime pay,' Julie said.

'I did, but I also bought some new speakers, plus there was an installation fee. It all came to nearly £500 and I didn't have the extra money so I put the whole thing on VISA.'

'What happened to the money you had for the stereo?' Mr Woods asked.

'I kept it, planning to use that to pay the VISA bill,' Paul replied. 'But somehow it was all spent before the bill arrived.'

'So now we owe another £500 on the VISA?' Julie shouted as the tears welled up in her eyes.

'Julie, please calm down,' Mr Woods said in a gentle voice. 'We knew the situation was bad or you wouldn't have come here. But I appreciate Paul's honesty about the debts. I can't be of any help to you if I don't know the entire situation.' As I see it, you have some pressing debts that have to be dealt with rather quickly. When you decided to make an IVA you made an agreement not to incur any additional debts. Now you have an additional £1500 of debt that your original creditors don't know about. The first thing you need to do is deal with that situation. I assume you don't have any surplus funds that can be used to pay these bills, do you?'

'No,' Paul replied. 'Only what's in the bank account, which isn't much at the moment.'

'You'll need that for normal living expenses,' Mr Woods said. 'Do you have any surplus in your account, Julie?'

Julie sat silently for several moments before she spoke. 'Yes, I do. But I don't want to use it to pay for Paul's indulgences.'

'I can understand that,' Mr Woods said. 'But if you're going to work out this situation and find a permanent solution, it will be because you do it together, working as one unit. If you're holding the money as a nest egg in case the marriage doesn't work, it won't. Satan would like nothing better than to drive a wedge between you and Paul, and God can only work in your marriage if you make an irrevocable commitment to make it work. Just as God will not listen to a husband who ignores his wife's advice, he also won't listen to a wife who rebels against her husband's authority.'

'But Paul doesn't take the leadership in our home,' Julie protested. 'So am I supposed to turn over all the money to him knowing that it will be spent foolishly?'

'No,' Mr Woods replied. 'The way to balance one extreme is not to go to the other. God put you two together because you need the balance that each offers the other. You must work together as one. Now is your chance to decide whether you trust God or just say that you trust God.

'Anyone can help you manage the money and pay the bills. That's a matter of following a plan I'll outline for you. But the financial problems you have are really a symptom of greater problems that exist. So unless you deal with the root problems, the symptoms will always return. Since the problems are spiritual in nature, only God can cure them.

'The Lord told us that no one can serve both God and money. The same is true in a marriage relationship. No couple can keep their assets separated and be one. There are some risks when you totally surrender your rights, but there are also some big rewards.

'Julie, I can't tell you what to do. All I can do is offer you advice based on what I believe God would have both of you do. I want you each to take some time to think and pray about your decisions. Call me when you have made a decision, and we'll get back together.

'In the meantime, Paul, I want you to contact the manager of the garage that has the bill on your car and tell him that we're working out a plan and will be in contact with him in the next two weeks. But you'll have to pay at least the minimum on the VISA bill or your IVA will be in jeopardy.'

During the next few days Julie hardly spoke to Paul. He tried to be as helpful as possible by doing things around the house and looking after Timothy in the evenings, but she found herself in a total state of confusion. She had separated herself from Paul financially, if not physically. She considered what Mr Woods had said about their problems being spiritual rather than financial. Inside she knew he was right. She had drifted so far from the Lord that she had begun to wonder if she really was a Christian. It was as if her faith had crumbled at the first test she had ever faced.

Finally, she made the decision to cross the invisible line back into her marriage. She vowed to God that she would commit her resources to her marriage and work at becoming one with Paul. She also knew that for the time being she had to give up her personal goals of finishing college and having a career. She would work at her marriage and learn to be content with whatever was God's will for her life. Suddenly she felt free, as if a great burden had been lifted from her shoulders.

She could hardly wait to get home to tell Paul about her decision. She arrived home before him and was sorting through the post. There was an official-looking envelope from the Inland Revenue. Her stomach did such a flip that she thought she might throw up. She sank down in one of the dining room chairs and just stared at the envelope for several minutes. She wasn't sure she even wanted to know what it said. She suspected that Paul hadn't completed his tax form and they were being investigated.

She put the envelope down and slid out of the chair to her knees. Resting her elbows on the chair seat, she closed her eyes and began to pray. 'Dear God, I know I'm living in fear and dread over our finances. I ask you to forgive my attitude and give me the peace that you promised. I know I have not been following your path or living by your plan, but I commit myself to you and to my husband, whatever the circumstances are.'

She stood up and picking up the envelope, started to open it. 'No,' she thought, 'I'll wait and let Paul open it. We'll face whatever it is together.' She dropped the letter on the table and began to make the dinner.

Paul came home a few minutes later. 'Hi, darling, how was your day?' he asked cheerfully. 'I had a good day,' Julie replied and gave Paul a hug.

Paul was shocked by her sudden display of affection. It had been several months since she had even kissed him voluntarily. Their physical relationship had deteriorated to the point where Paul was afraid to show any affection, for fear she would totally reject him.

'Paul, I know I've been depressed and moody about our finances recently,' Julie confessed.

'It's not your fault,' Paul replied. 'I've given you plenty of cause to be worried, but I am committed to making a change. I want to be a good husband with God's help.'

'Hush, Paul, and let me say what I want to say first. It doesn't matter about the problems anymore. We'll work them out together as long as you'll let me help. I have decided to close my bank account and put the money into our joint account. I have about £500 and I want you to use it to pay off some of the debts.'

'I can't do that,' Paul protested. 'That money is yours. It seems like somebody else always has to clean up my mess.'

'No, you're wrong. The money is not mine,' Julie said emphatically. 'It's not really even ours. It belongs to God. We seem to have forgotten that somewhere along the way. I want the money in my account to be used for our expenses.'

They just stood there for several minutes holding each other. Then Julie said, 'Paul, a letter came from the tax man today. I didn't want to open it so I left it on the table.'

'Oh no, what now?' Paul said as he picked up the envelope

from the table. 'I know we don't owe any money to the Inland Revenue, at least I hope we don't.' Opening the envelope Paul let out a whoop. 'Julie, we don't owe any money! This is a cheque for nearly £900.'

'Why did they send us a cheque?' Julie asked as she began to relax her body from the shock she had expected.

'The letter says that we overpaid our taxes because of a computer error. Well, praise the Lord! With this we'll be able to pay off the debts and still have some of your money left. Let's go out and celebrate tonight.'

'Oh, no,' Julie responded. 'That's the kind of thinking that got us into this mess in the first place.'

'Just joking,' Paul said with a big grin. 'I would much rather stay at home and celebrate with my family.'

Two weeks later Paul and Julie were back in Mr Woods' office. 'Well, I'm glad to see you back again,' he began. 'Obviously your presence here means you have decided to work together on your financial problems. I'll be honest with you. About half of the couples the minister sends to me don't ever come back. They are looking for either a guaranteed miracle or some kind of quick fix. But if you didn't get into debt in three months, you won't get out of debt in three months. And as far as miracles go, I have seen God move in miraculous ways, but the more common approach is that he allows those who violate his principles to work their way out. Somehow the lessons seem to stick a lot better that way.'

'We're not looking for a miracle or a quick fix,' said Paul. 'I know I created this mess by my own ignorance and childishness. I'm willing to do whatever is necessary to solve this once and for all.'

'What about you, Julie?' Mr Woods asked.

'I'm committed to the Lord, my husband, and whatever else it takes, in that order,' Julie said confidently. 'I have already closed my account and put the surplus into our joint account.'

'Good for you. I believe Paul is going to be worthy of your

trust, and I know God will honour your faith. Now let's get down to business.'

'First, we would like to ask a couple of questions,' Paul said.

'Certainly. What would you like to ask?'

'As you may have guessed, we haven't been attending a church regularly for the past year or so. But we made a commitment to join Pastor Hurley's church last week. Julie feels very strongly that we should begin to tithe again. I want to, but I can't work out where the money would come from, even with the two new debts paid. Can we tithe even if it means we can't meet the obligations of the IVA?'

'I commend your commitment to join a good church and to tithe, but when you made a proposal to your creditors you entered into a binding agreement. You can't legally break your commitment and continue the IVA. As I see it you have two choices. You can elect to come out of the IVA and take your chances with your creditors. Or you can reduce your own living expenses to where you can tithe and still meet your obligations.'

'How can we do that?' Paul asked. 'There is no extra money available, except the small amount Julie was saving, but even that should go to buy some clothes for Timothy and her.'

'I think we're jumping ahead a little here. Let me tell you what I think, and maybe some questions will be answered. First, your combined incomes are approximately £2,400 a month, is that right?'

'Yes,' Paul replied. 'That's pretty close.'

'And your net take-home pay is about £1,800?'

'I don't really know,' Paul replied.

'Yes it is,' Julie chimed in.

'OK,' Mr Woods said. I calculate your overall housing expense to be around £1,000 a month. That means it takes nearly fifty-five per cent of your total spendable income just to maintain your home. That's at least twenty per cent too high for your income. Even if you tithed, housing should never cost more than forty per cent of your spendable income after tithing.'

'I was convinced all along that our home cost us too much,' Julie said. 'But I didn't know how to calculate what we could afford. The bank used twenty-five per cent of our total incomes when we bought the house. But I was making more money then.'

'Gross income doesn't mean a thing,' Mr Woods said. 'It's what you have left over to spend that's important.'

'Are you saying that we should sell our home and move to a cheaper one?' Paul asked.

'I'm not going to tell you to do anything,' Mr Woods replied. 'I'm just going to point out some logical alternatives, then you'll have to make your own choices. I know that usually the wife is attached to her home and giving it up is a difficult decision.'

'Not for me,' Julie said quickly. 'I have always viewed that house as a weight around our necks. It was Paul who really wanted it in the first place.'

'That's probably true,' Paul said. 'But the chaps at work said it was stupid to pay rent when I could buy a home and get all the tax advantages.'

'Usually that's pretty good logic, but not when you wreck your budget to buy. It would be better to rent and stay within your income, than to buy and end up in debt,' Mr Woods said. 'I believe that potentially you could free up about £400 a month by renting for a while.'

'Four hundred pounds a month!' exclaimed Paul. 'That's enough to pay our tithe and more. I just never realised the house was putting us into debt. I always thought of it as a good long-term investment.'

'For most families it is. But only after they have settled into a lifestyle and found a home within their budget. Buying a home too quickly and one that is too expensive is the number one reason why most young couples end up in financial trouble. And since about forty per cent end up in divorce, the home will eventually be sold anyway.'

'But why doesn't someone tell young couples these things before they make the mistakes we made?' Julie asked.

'In our society people make money off the excesses of others, unfortunately. But in Proverbs 24:27 God does present the principle I'm talking about: "Finish your outdoor work and get your fields ready; after that, build your house".'

'I've never heard that before,' Paul said in amazement. 'I'll put the house up for sale today.'

'Hold on just a minute, Paul,' Mr Woods said. 'Don't do anything in haste. Pray about the decision first, and ask God to bring the right buyer for your home. You need to think about some other areas, too. I'm going to give you a workbook that will help you plan each area of your budget. It's especially important that you allocate money for non-monthly expenses such as clothes, car maintenance and annual insurance. These are normally the areas that create crisis when they are due.'

'That's certainly true in our case,' Julie said.

'We want your budget to be totally realistic, or it will only work for a short while. You're going to be tight on money for another year and a half, until all your debts are paid. But with some discipline you will be debt-free in less than two years.

'I have one additional recommendation for you. I believe Julie is far better equipped to maintain the records and pay the bills. The short personality test I gave you last time shows that she is a detail person, while you, Paul, are a generalist.'

'I would agree with that,' Paul said. 'But I have always been taught that it is the man's responsibility to run the finances in his family.'

'Paul, God gives each of us gifts and abilities to help us in our daily lives. It's clear that Julie is better suited to be the bookkeeper in your family. The two of you together need to work out a financial plan and then she will pay the bills and maintain the records. God doesn't make mistakes; he provided the necessary talents in Julie that you lack, and vice versa. I suggest that you read Proverbs 31 together, because it describes a husband and wife working as a team. It's clear that each uses different and unique abilities to enhance the relationship.

'Our short-term goal will be to get your finances to the point where you're able to pay everyone what you owe them each month. That will mean Julie will need to continue to work, at least for a while, but our long-term goal will be to free you financially so that Julie does not have to work.'

'But we have tried that before. Every time I stopped working we fell further and further behind,' Julie said.

'That's because you started out with expenses larger than your income. I believe you'll find when you readjust your budget that you'll be able to get by on one income. Later, if you want to work, you should use your income for one-time purchases.'

'What do you mean?' asked Paul.

'Save it up and buy a car, or save it for a down payment on a home, but don't commit yourselves to monthly expenses based on two incomes, especially at your age. If you do, something as normally exciting as a child can end up being the source of grief and conflict,'

'That's true,' Paul replied, looking at Julie.

'I want you both to go home with the plan I have given you and make the necessary adjustments in your budget. Remember that each and every category of spending must have some money allocated to it. To ignore areas like entertainment and recreation is unrealistic and will cause your budget to fail within a short period of time. Ignoring needs like clothing, car repairs and dental bills will make your budget look good but will also make it totally unrealistic.'

'What about the tithing?' Julie asked. 'I always tithed before I was married, but we have been unable to for most of our marriage.'

'Tithing is an important principle for a Christian because it demonstrates a commitment to God in the most visible area of our lives: the area of money. But God wants you to honour your word also. You have made an agreement to pay your creditors according to the budget you submitted, so you must do so. One part of your long-term plan should be to reduce your monthly expenses so that you can give God his portion, too. But for now you'll have to stick to the plan you have. I believe God will honour the commitment of your heart. He doesn't care about the money nearly as much as he cares about your heart's attitude. Tithing will be a part of the next stage of financial planning for you and Paul once the expenses are reduced.'

CHAPTER 9

DEVELOP AND CARRY OUT
A PLAN FOR PAYING OFF DEBTS

We trust that by now you recognise the errors that Paul and Julie made in their finances. Their problem could be called 'too much, too soon'. It is a common mistake for many young couples in our society. It has been said (and, unfortunately, it is all too true) that a young couple today tries to accumulate in three years what it took their parents thirty years to accumulate. The one thing couples need to learn very quickly is that individuals must be self-disciplined today. They cannot count on the lenders to force them to live within their means, as they once did.

Prior to the late sixties bankers were among the most conservative people in our society. Before anyone could borrow for consumables such as food or clothes, or even for non-consumables such as cars and houses, his financial status was thoroughly reviewed, and formulas were applied to ensure his borrowing stayed within his means to repay. This is not true today. The increasing demand to make more loans has widened the parameters of acceptable loans. It is now assumed that the borrowers will discipline themselves to repay what they borrow. Unfortunately, many young couples have no idea how to calculate what they can or cannot afford to pay.

More than sixty per cent of all first-time home loans require two salaries to make the payments. But since the vast majority of first-time home buyers are couples under thirty-five years old, the prospect of a baby disrupting their cash flow is almost a certainty. So they have built-in potential financial problems from the start. Combine that with the use of second mortgages to help make the down payments and loans for refrigerators, carpets and curtains, and you can see why so many young couples end up in financial trouble.

But the main purpose of this book is not to show how most people get into debt, but rather to help you understand how to get out of debt. To do that, we need to follow Paul and Julie as they go through the plan Mr Woods worked out for them.

First, it is important to understand that by the time they went to Mr Woods they were deeply in debt and had elected to pay their creditors through an IVA. Table 9.1 is a summary of Paul and Julie's financial condition when Mr Woods first saw them. The figures on the left reflect what an average family in their salary range would normally spend in a month on various household expenses. The figures on the right reflect what Paul and Julie had budgeted.

As you can see, Paul and Julie had a financial problem that could be solved only by creating more income or by spending less. Since more income wasn't an option for them, they had to spend less.

In reality, spending less is the answer for the vast majority of debt problems. Most of us would be able to spend almost unlimited amounts of money, given the chance. So more money coming in usually means more money going out. Remember that Paul had already tried a debt consolidation loan through his bank. Usually that helps for a short while because the monthly payments are reduced through a lower interest, longer-term loan. But unless the conditions that caused the initial problems are changed, the end result will be even more debt. In Paul's case, he had to pay back not only the consolidation loan, but also the credit card bills he had built up a few months later, so he was actually worse off than he was before he got the consolidation loan.

Table 9.1
Paul and Julie Elvers' 'As Is' Budget
Compared to a Recommended Spending Plan
for a Family with a Monthly Income of £1800 Net

Average Spending		The Elvers' 'As Is' Budget	
Taxes	(taken out)	Taxes	(taken out)
Tithe	180.00	Tithe	0.00
Housing	567.00	Housing	1,080.00
Cars	240.00	Cars	280.00
Food	280.00	Food	200.00
Clothing	80.00	Clothing	0.00
Insurance	80.00	Insurance	0.00
Ent & Recreation	95.00	Ent & Recreation	25.00
Debt	80.00	Debt	250.00
Miscellaneous	100.00	Miscellaneous	25.00
Savings	80.00	Savings	0.00
Total	£1,782.00	Total	£1,860.00

A glance at the Elvers' 'as is' budget tells much of the story. Their budget could have handled the spending of 30 to 35 percent of the net pay for housing (about £500 per month) but they had committed themselves to payments that were nearly 60 percent of their income, or £840 per month. When utilities were added their expenses for housing came to more than £1,000. They could not make it on such a budget, even from the beginning. They were running at a deficit from the time they made the first mortgage payment until the home was sold.

Note also that they were overcommitted in the categories of cars and outstanding debt. Those debts were the obvious result of lack of money created each month by the high housing payments. When necessities came up – such as clothes, insurance or car repairs – Paul used credit to make up the difference. The overcommitment he made regarding the cars reflected Paul's weakness for cars. This is quite common in young men as they see their car as a personal status symbol. This is a poor attitude, even when single, but it can lead to disaster when the young man gets married and continues to cling to the same values.

When you look at the budget for clothing, entertainment and insurance, you will note that Paul and Julie allocated nothing on a regular monthly basis for these items. That does not mean that they found a miraculous way to keep their clothes from wearing out, or that they never went to see a film or had a meal out. It means they did not have money for these items so they left them out of their budget. When they incurred these expenses – as they were bound to – Paul and Julie had to rely on credit cards to make up the deficit. That is why so many couples say they use their credit cards only for necessities. Often that's true because other spending creates the need to use the cards for the necessities.

Mr Woods gave Paul and Julie some suggestions to help them resolve both their immediate and their long-term problems.

1. Use the funds they already had on hand to pay the VISA bill and the outstanding balance on the car Paul had returned. Mr Woods made direct contact with the owner of the car showroom and told him what had happened with Paul. The owner agreed to accept a reduced amount in total payment of the bill which saved Paul £300.
2. Each month continue to meet the obligations agreed with the creditors. With Paul and Julie's combined incomes they were able to pay at least the minimum amounts due.
3. Make a budget showing what they could afford to pay for housing, assuming that their debts were paid and they had only Paul's income. This showed how totally out of line their housing expenses were with their income. They decided to sell the house and find housing that would meet their needs.

4. Assign Julie the task of managing the books in their home. She would pay the bills each month and she and Paul would review the budget together at least once a month.

5. Make a budget that they could live with once the IVA was completed and assume in that budget that they would have only Paul's income to work with and that they would be repaying – in total – everyone to whom they owed money.

The budget shown in Table 9.2 is the Elvers' 'want to' budget. It shows where Paul and Julie wanted to be when the IVA was cleared. Note the reduced amount for housing, which is a much more realistic figure for Paul's income. The new spending plan meant that Paul and Julie had to give up their home and rent for a period of time. But that was a small sacrifice compared with the peace of mind they had lost when they committed themselves to buying that home.

Table 9.2
'Want to' Budget for Paul and Julie Elvers
Based on an After Tax Income of £1,400 Per Month

Taxes	(taken out)
Tithe	150.00
Housing	450.00
Car	200.00
Food	250.00
Clothes	50.00
Insurance	70.00
Ent. & Recreation	100.00
Debt	0.00
Miscellaneous	60.00
Savings	70.00
Total	£1,400.00

Also note that they committed the first portion of their income to God as a tithe. They prayed about repaying God's portion and, once the last creditor was repaid, used Julie's income for several months to repay their tithes. Mr Woods told them that as far as he could tell Scripture did not require or suggest a repayment of past tithes and offerings. After praying about what he said, they still committed themselves to repaying their tithes as a testimony that God truly was first in their marriage.

Paul and Julie had some questions about their situation that are common to couples in their position. We thought it might be helpful to others to review those questions.

What effect will the IVA or bankruptcy have on our future credit?

Any credit reference agency can report that you have entered into an IVA or bankruptcy for up to six years after the date of that action. Therefore, any potential lender enquiring about your credit history will receive that report.

Is there any way to clear our credit rating?

Not really. Too often in our society people act as if there are no consequences of not paying debts but that is simply not true. The bankruptcy laws were originally created to help balance an unjust system that sent poor people to prison for bad debts. But too often today they are abused by people who don't want to repay money they have already spent. Consequently, legitimate creditors look upon those who use bankruptcy as people who don't want to pay their bills. The net effect is that those who go bankrupt are often refused credit from legitimate lenders later.

Is there any way we can prove that we are honest and re-establish a good credit rating?

Yes. Once the IVA is cleared you can continue to pay the entirety of the debts you owe. After a creditor is completely paid off ask him to write you a letter of recommendation and send a copy to his credit reference agency. An agency may include letters of recommendation in their official credit reports. But you can also give the letters to a potential lender when you apply for a loan yourself.

The best recommendation we can give to anyone is this: pay back what you borrow and never borrow frivolously. Remember what Proverbs 22:1 says: 'A good name is more desirable than great riches; to be esteemed is better than silver or gold.' A summary of how credit reference agencies work is to be found at the end of this book.

What would happen if Paul lost his job for any reason?

You should notify your IVA Supervisor immediately. Usually they will try to work out a temporary arrangement with your creditors. However, if the situation lasts for any extended period of time, bankruptcy may become the only option. In other words, your assets are sold and the creditors paid with the proceeds from the sale.

Anyone who is not in an IVA needs to stay in direct contact with his creditors and tell them the absolute truth. Most creditors will work with a debtor who has temporary financial problems as long as he is trying to be fair and honest.

CHAPTER 10

COMMON ERRORS
THAT LEAD TO DEBT

There are fundamental biblical principles that, if violated, ultimately result in financial disaster. One is allowing a get-rich-quick mentality to control your decisions. Symptoms of get-rich-quick are evident in many of the investment schemes in this country and around the world today. There are three distinguishing characteristics.

Risking borrowed money

If investments in get-rich-quick schemes were limited to available cash only, most people would be wary of losing it. But somehow it is easier to risk borrowed money because it seems almost free – at least until you have to pay it back. The same principle applies to buying consumer goods on credit. Credit card companies understand the mentality of over-indulging on purchases bought with borrowed money. People who use their credit cards for clothes, food and holidays are prime candidates for over-buying. Credit card issuers can prove to a store statistically that those people will buy more and pay a higher price than those who buy only with cash.

There is no argument that through the use of borrowed money you can get rich a lot faster. But there is also no argument that the majority of those who do so, end up losing it all in the long run, for the mentality that prompted them to take the initial risk will prompt them to take ever bigger risks – and eventually they will get wiped out in a bad economy. As the proverb says, 'The plans of the diligent lead to profit as surely as haste leads to poverty' (Prov 21:5).

You don't have to look any further than the oil industry to verify that principle. Many multi-millionaires were totally wiped out between 1983 and 1985 when the price of oil dropped precipitously. But it wasn't the price of oil that destroyed them. It was the fact that they had borrowed against everything they owned to expand their investments. When the bottom fell out of the market, as it always does eventually, they lost everything.

Getting involved in things you don't understand

The second element of the get-rich-quick mentality – taking financial risks in fields you know little or nothing about – is dangerous if there is any possibility of losing sizeable amounts of money in the investment. It would be difficult to convince a chemist to invest large amounts of borrowed money in a scheme to turn lead into gold. A chemist understands the physics of the elements too well to be trapped by such a wild scheme (usually!). So the logical candidate for such a venture is a businessman who has made his fortune in frozen pizzas. He knows pizzas well, but knows nothing at all about the molecular structure of lead and gold. Obviously, you won't find every pizza baron investing in lead-to-gold conversion schemes, but you definitely shouldn't find any chemists doing it.

But Christians are particularly vulnerable to being tricked by foolish schemes because they tend to trust anyone who calls himself a Christian, especially if he claims to have a special 'revelation' from God. Beware of anyone who is selling something and says, 'I was praying about this idea and God told me to call you.' If that person really is a prophet of the Lord, ask him to give a couple of short-term prophecies that you can verify before you put your trust in him.

The lesson to be learned is this: stay with what you know best, and you'll lose a lot less money in the long run.

Ignoring the main adviser the Lord has provided

It is very dangerous for a husband or wife to ignore the adviser the Lord has provided in his or her partner. In his infinite wisdom, God created humankind as male and female. He didn't have to. After all, he did create asexual creatures who have no need of a mate or a friend. But we suspect they lead rather dull lives.

When you live with someone in a relationship as close as husband and wife, there are bound to be problems. Since opposites tend to attract, you won't agree about everything. In fact, you may never totally agree about anything. But that's OK, as long as you know how to work it out together and reach a reasonable compromise.

Often it is not the person from a wealthy background who is obsessed by success, but rather the one from a modest or poor background. We all have the tendency to over-compensate for what we lacked as children.

These distinctives in personality types should not be ignored when a couple works out the decision-making function in their marriage. We Christians have stereotyped the roles of husband and wife based on what the apostle Paul taught about roles of leadership in the organised church. When we do that we ignore the totality of God's word on the subject and fail to recognise psychological realities.

The Scriptures do not draw an exact parallel between home relationships and the church. Instead, when the totality of God's word is considered, and not just isolated passages, it is evident that mutual decision-making is a more accurate description of the Bible's advice on the matter. Genesis 2:24 indicates that the woman is to have the role of helpmate in the marriage. In 1 Peter 3:7 the husband is warned to treat his wife with grace and honour, lest his 'prayers be hindered'. When a husband avoids or ignores his wife's advice on any matter, including finances, he should expect his prayers to be hindered. The same can be said for a wife who does not give her husband the respect that God has assigned him as head of the family.

God created husband and wife to function as a single working unit, each with different but essential abilities. Certainly those abilities will overlap in many areas, and often that will lead to differences of opinion. But just as certainly, without the balance that each can bring to the marriage, great errors in judgement will be made.

It has been our observation that a dominant woman operating on her own initiative will accumulate debt through credit cards and store cards because she buys too many clothes or too much furniture. A dominant husband operating on his own initiative will accumulate debt through the purchase of houses and cars and other investments. Men don't buy very often, but when they do, they buy big.

Facing bankruptcy with prudence and honour

Bankruptcy may well be the result of a failed get-rich-quick scheme. In most instances action by any major creditor is sufficient to force a bankruptcy. A bankruptcy will usually provide only a fraction of the total debt owed to creditors, but creditors are required to accept the liquidation proceeds as total settlement of their debt.

CHAPTER 11

LEARN TO LIVE WITHIN A FINANCIAL PLAN

The financial troubles of the second couple discussed in this book, John and Mary Thompson, look at first as though they were the result of circumstances the couple could not control. Surely no one could have foreseen the medical problems their son would have. It could be argued that the additional expenses and the fact that Mary was unable to return to work would have wrecked anyone's budget.

But the fact is that John and Mary's financial troubles were the result of poor planning. Although they were intelligent and committed people they had never been taught the basics of finances. They had never measured John's income against normal monthly expenses and they had made no provision for any emergency spending they might one day have to make. The only way the couple could manage financially was to use Mary's income to balance the budget. This basic fact was not obvious to John and Mary, and as a consequence the steps they took as they began to slip into debt only made a bad situation worse.

Shortly after the baby was born John and Mary's church took up a collection to help them with the additional expenses, but the extent of their debts was far beyond the means of a small church. The couple found they were unable to meet their mortgage repayments and the repayments on a small debt on some furniture they had purchased. But since they had no real budget, they naturally assumed their financial problems were the result of the baby's problems and Mary's inability to keep working.

They soon developed an 'I don't care' mentality about their finances. They assumed the situation was hopeless. Though they continued to pray about their needs, they adopted the attitude of many Christians: they prayed and assumed God wouldn't answer.

They began to use their credit cards to fill the gaps in their budget. John bought his petrol on credit and ate out on credit, while Mary bought baby supplies and food on credit. Without realising it, they had adopted an attitude of despair and a philosophy that bankruptcy was inevitable. As is common, they were holding a pity party at their creditors' expense. With no visible means to repay, they were running up bills and living beyond their means. Although John would never have robbed a bank, he was in effect doing the same thing – stealing from his creditors.

Seven months after the baby was born, the couple were beginning to reap the seeds they had sown. Creditors were telephoning daily because nearly all their bills were outstanding. Two credit card companies had filed judgements against them – which John had ignored because he felt there was nothing that could be done anyway. When an attachment of earnings order was put on his salary he was called into the school administrator's office.

'John, I have received a notice of attachment from the court,' Mr Mills said solemnly. 'I have to comply with the request and withhold twenty per cent of your net pay. Do you have financial problems?'

'Yes,' John responded a little defiantly. 'It's because of the baby.'

'We know things must have been difficult for you and Mary, and we're working on something that might help. But the attachment is the result of a judgement from a

VISA bill. Are these debts related to the baby?'

'No, not directly,' John said, looking down at the floor as he spoke. 'We've had to use our credit cards for normal expenses during the last few months, but it all started because of the baby's problems.'

Then Mr Mills began to realise that John had allowed the problems with the baby to distort his thinking. He said, 'John I believe your problems are far greater than those caused by the baby. I know we don't pay our teachers nearly enough and it's tough to manage on one salary. But you took the job knowing that, and now I suspect that even without the baby you would be in over your head. I want you to go to a debt counsellor and get a clear picture of where you are financially.'

'Will I lose my job because of this?' John asked.

'No,' Mr Mills responded. 'We have neither the right nor the authority to dismiss you for that reason. But with Mary not working, you would have a difficult time making ends meet, even if all your finances were in perfect order. We do have some teachers supporting families on one salary, but they must be very careful and live on a strict budget. With this attachment I know you won't be able to manage. Do you have other debts besides the VISA?'

'Well, yes, we do,' John responded uncomfortably.

'More than a thousand pounds?'

'Well, yes, I suppose so. But we have decided to file for bankruptcy anyway because we just can't live on my salary and repay our debts,' John said with an air of finality.

'No one would argue with that,' Mr Mills said as he recognised John's defensiveness. 'John, as Christians, and more so as teachers, you and I have a responsibility to demonstrate the attributes of Jesus to those around us. In the eyes of our generation, nothing is as visible as the way we handle our finances.'

'I agree,' John said, interrupting. 'But God must have known that our baby would need a lot of attention and cost us a great deal. Who's to say this is not his plan?'

'I would. And I would say that even if our roles were reversed and it was my son with the health problems. I believe you have allowed your circumstances to overrule your first commitment – to the Lord.'

'That's easy for you to say, because it isn't your son, and you make more money than I do,' John said defiantly.

'That's very true. But I would hope that our faith is not built on what someone else does or doesn't have, or on what they would or wouldn't do in similar circumstances. You see, there will always be someone else who is better off than either of us and someone who will have more money than both of us.'

Again John said, 'That's easy enough to say when it's not your finances. But I don't see anyone paying our bills for us.'

'Perhaps that is not entirely true, John.'

'What do you mean?'

'Several members of the school board and the faculty have put money into your account over the last couple of months to help pay off some of your debts, because we realise that you can't meet all your expenses. Didn't you notice that your account had more money in it than it should have?'

John stopped cold. No, he hadn't noticed. He had been so caught up in his problems that he had taken an antagonistic stance in relation to most of the creditors and had ignored all their correspondence. Mary had commented several times that they should try to contact the major creditors and let them know that they were having some severe financial problems. John had shrugged it off saying, 'We can't pay them anyway. So what difference does it make?'

John was taken aback. 'I don't know what to say.'

'You don't need to say anything. We did what we did because we care. But now I fear your situation is serious and you and Mary need to pray about what to do. But let me encourage you to seek good advice and not to listen to the advice of those who look for the easy way out all the time.'

Reality began to set in. John was excited about going home

and telling Mary about the money that had been paid into their account, but as he drove home a feeling of depression came over him. He realised that they would still owe hundreds of pounds on credit cards that they had used over the last few months. He began to accept the fact that they would be paying for their ignorance and lack of self-discipline, perhaps for years.

Mary wasn't at home when John arrived, so he decided to review some of the bills that had been sent during the last few weeks. Most of them were still in his desk drawer unopened. He opened the envelopes and began to sort the bills by date and amount. An hour passed as he sorted bills from the utility companies, store cards and three major credit cards. When he added up what he had found he was shocked. 'Surely this must be some kind of mistake,' John told himself. 'We can't possibly owe that much.' Yet when he retotalled the pile of bills, the figure came out the same: £6,763.34. Almost £7,000! And he knew that he still hadn't found all the bills. He had been so sure they only owed a few hundred pounds that even £1,000 would have been a shock. But £7,000. It seemed impossible.

When Mary arrived home she knew immediately that something was wrong. John was still sitting at the desk looking at the pile of bills in front of him. 'What's the problem?' she asked, not really wanting to know.

'Mr Mills told me today that members of the school board have been paying money into our account to try to help clear our debts.'

'Well, surely that's good news,' Mary responded enthusiastically. 'But what's the problem?'

'I have just added up the debts. We owe nearly £7,000 and I know that's not all of it.'

'That's impossible,' Mary nearly shouted.

'Unfortunately, it's not. We also have a judgement against my wages, as of today. I feel so stupid, Mary. I've been living as if there were no tomorrow and no God. I suppose I just assumed we would have to go bankrupt, so I didn't care how much debt we ran up. God has been faithful to fulfil his part but I failed to do my part.'

'What is the alternative now?' Mary asked as she moved to put Thomas in his cot.

'I believe we have only one. God stopped us from filing for bankruptcy by removing any excuse we might have had. The debts we owe are as a result of our own decisions, and I can't blame anyone but myself. I don't see how we can do anything but commit ourselves to paying off our debts.'

'But how will we be able to do that on your salary alone?' Mary asked.

'I don't think we can. I'll just have to tell Mr Mills that I need to start looking for a new job. In the meantime I'll go to each of the creditors and ask for a reduced payment until I can generate more income. But we can't do anything about the attachment. That will come directly out of my salary until the debt is paid in full. It won't leave us a lot to live on, but we'll have to learn to do it.'

'I want to cut up the credit cards too. As long as we have them we'll be tempted to use them. And I think we need to go back to one car. Maybe we can sell my car for enough to clear the VISA and the attachment.'

'But my car has nearly one hundred thousand miles on the clock. Can we manage with a car that old?'

'We'll have to. It's going to be tough for a while, but we'll just have to do it.'

John left the Christian school for a job as a teacher and coach at a state school. He and Mary went to see the debt counsellor Mr Mills had suggested and worked out a plan with their creditors that allowed them some transition time. It was nearly two years before they began to see daylight at the end of the tunnel, but in three years they were totally debt-free.

They began teaching a course on finances in their church and are still teaching it. Before any young couple can get married in their church they must sit through a six-hour course on how to manage money God's way. John's desire is to one day be the head of a school where he can influence young people before they make the mistakes he did.

CHAPTER 12

ACCEPT RESPONSIBILITY FOR YOUR LIFE

In this chapter we will look at another couple, Bill and Pam. They were both in their early twenties and at university. They were both Christians, although from different ends of the spectrum philosophically. Bill came from a more traditional background. This difference in their church backgrounds is referred to only because of the influence that the teaching they received in their churches had on their decisions.

Both came from middle-class homes with parents who were Christians. Throughout their time at school they had not received any teaching on how to handle money, and although they had both worked in a variety of summer jobs for several years, neither had more than a vague idea of how to balance a cheque book.

They had met at a rally held by the Christian union and had started going out together. Both Pam and Bill had struggled through college on a student grant and student loans and by the time they were in their final year they each had debts of around £3,000. In the early part of her final year, Pam's father died of a sudden heart attack. Her mother was devastated by her loss and went into a prolonged state of depression. Pam dropped out of college for one term and then returned to finish her degree. In the past, her father had always given her money for the incidentals she needed, but now she had to ask her mother.

'Mum, I'll need some money for books and other bits and pieces,' she said.

'Dad always handled the finances, sweetheart. I don't know what you need. Why don't you take my credit card and get whatever you need and we'll work it out when you come home next time. Maybe Dad's affairs will be settled by that time and I'll know what we have.' Pam's mum handed over her credit card. Although Pam had never owned a card of her own, she had often used her mother's to fill up the family car or run errands for her mum. The card had only her mother's initials and last name on it. Because Pam had the same initials as her mother, her signature had never been questioned.

Back at college she called her mum almost daily on a mobile phone she had purchased with the credit card. When the first bill came it was nearly £200, which she paid with her mother's card. She needed some clothes and normally would have asked her dad for some money. Usually he sent her about £100 and she would buy a pair of jeans and a couple of blouses. Since she thought her mother wouldn't want to be bothered about new clothes, she decided to use the card. By the time she had finished the shopping trip she had charged almost £500 on the card. £120 of that was spent on a watch for Bill.

She and Bill began to talk seriously about their plans after graduation. They knew they would get married, but beyond that they had no definite plans about what they would do. Bill was working towards a degree in music and Pam hoped to get a teaching job in a local school.

Over the next few months Pam fell into the habit of using her mother's credit card periodically for little luxuries. None were particularly significant by themselves, but when added up they began to be significant. The bills were sent to her mother who put them in her desk unopened. She was still depressed and just couldn't cope with the details of daily life.

Suddenly Pam saw college coming to an end and was faced with entering the work force for the first time. She began to feel a little panicky. She thought more and more about getting married. She feared that if they waited until summer, something might happen to keep them from getting married. That thought really panicked her. She had lost her father; she couldn't stand the thought of possibly losing Bill too.

One evening she said to Bill, 'Why don't we just go ahead and get married? I know Mum couldn't cope with organising a wedding at the moment, and I'm not sure that emotionally she could cope with seeing me get married anyway.'

'But how will we cope financially?' Bill asked. 'Neither of us has a job.'

'We already have my flat,' Pam replied. 'And without your rent our expenses would actually be less, wouldn't they?'

'Well, I suppose so,' he replied as he thought about the idea. 'But I'm not sure that my dad would continue to help me out financially if we got married.'

'Well hopefully I'll get a job before too long.'

The more Bill thought about the idea, the more he liked it too. They had planned to get married that next summer anyway, so what difference would three or four months make? 'Besides,' he thought, 'Pam's right. Her mother is certainly in no state to organise a wedding.'

'I think it's a great idea,' he said as he put his arms around her. 'When would you like to get married?'

'What about Saturday,' she said.

'Saturday,' Bill echoed. 'Surely we need to wait longer than that?'

'No, we can get married by special licence. If we see the registrar today, there only has to be one clear day before we can get married, and then we can have a nice weekend away.'

'But how will we afford it?' he asked.

'I've got my credit cards,' she replied eagerly. 'There's a lovely hotel I've always wanted to stay in. I know it's expensive but it is such a special time.'

Bill had a nagging feeling inside about doing something so serious on impulse. He wondered what his mum would say when she found out. But seeing Pam so excited and knowing that they did love each other, he couldn't come up with a logical argument that would satisfy her. So he said, 'OK, Pam, we'll get married. You pack some things and I'll call my mum and let her know.'

Pam panicked inside as Bill mentioned calling his mum. 'Please don't tell anyone right now,' she pleaded. 'They'll just try to talk us out of it. I want this to be our surprise. We'll tell them after we have graduated, OK?'

Bill agreed reluctantly, but he knew his mum would be upset when she found out. Pam said, 'Let's just go straight away. We don't need any extra clothes. We'll only be gone a couple of days at the most, and we can buy something if we really need it.'

By this time Bill was totally into the idea as well, so he replied, 'This is really crazy, but if that's what you want, we'll do it. At least we'll have something to tell our grandchildren. But let's agree on one thing. No children until we're both settled into our jobs, OK?'

Pam agreed and grabbed Bill around the waist. 'We're going to be really happy, Bill. I just know it.'

Feeling excited they went to the registry office to get the licence and agreed to go to an Italian restaurant that evening to celebrate. They talked excitedly about their plans and had an extra special bottle of wine to toast their future. When the bill came, Pam gave the waitress her credit card and got a shock when she replied, 'Sorry, this is a cash only establishment.' They frantically searched their wallets and pockets and just managed to scrape together enough to pay the bill.

Saturday saw the wedding take place, followed by a weekend away at the hotel. The bill was much more than they had expected, but they were so happy in each other's company they just charged it to the credit card and forgot all about the expense.

A month later Pam's mother called her. 'Pam, I've been

looking through some of the bills and I have had a letter from the credit card company to say that I am over my limit. But I've hardly used that card and there is more than £2,000 charged to it.'

'£2,000! Mum, that's impossible,' Pam explained. 'I've used it for college expenses and some clothes, but I certainly didn't charge £2,000 to it.'

'There are charges on here from a very expensive hotel. Have you really been there?'

Pam sat quietly for a few seconds. She was overwhelmed by the news from her mother. She had put the hotel and the charges completely out of her mind during the last month. Being married was everything to her, and she and Bill had been very happy. But now she knew she had to tell her mother. 'Mum, Bill and I got married a month ago. That's where the charges came from. But don't worry, we'll pay you back.'

Pam's mother had suspected that something had been going on, but she was still shocked and hurt that they had not told her. She replied, 'That was your choice, but I wish you had at least let me know before you got married. Bill's mother is going to be very upset. But you'll have to work that out for yourselves, and now that you are married you will have to manage your own finances, so I'm sending all the bills to you. You'll have to take care of them.'

'But, Mum,' Pam pleaded, 'we don't have any money to pay all the bills just now.'

'I'm sorry, Pam, but you should have considered that before you got married and ran up all those debts.' With that, she hung up the phone.

Pam looked around the small room that served as their living area. There were several things that she had bought using the credit card, and she realised that she may well have charged up £2,000 or more. She had been using the card since they got married and was frightened as she realised that they may well have charged another several hundred pounds. Final exams were still five weeks away and they had no visible means of support. She decided not to tell Bill anything about what her mother had said until after the finals. He needed to concentrate on his exams and she knew he would worry himself sick about the debts. He already looked strained from concern about what he would tell his parents.

For nearly two weeks Pam tried diligently not to use the credit card for anything. Her mother had sent her the bills, and after looking through them she knew they were her charges. Then one evening, while Bill was studying, she got a call from his mother. 'Pam, is Bill there?' she asked.

Without thinking Pam replied, 'No, he's gone to the library to study.' There was a long pause on the other end of the line. Pam tried to think of something to say, but decided that this was as good a time as any for Bill's mother to find out.

'Are you and Bill living together?' Bill's mother asked with a measured calmness.

'Well, Mrs Yates, we got married about a month ago,' Pam replied. 'I'm sorry we didn't tell you, but we just didn't know how.'

'I rather suspected something was going on,' she said sternly. 'I do think you might have respected us enough to at least tell us your plans. But if you're married, you're married. So let's make the best of it. Please tell Bill to call me when he comes in. We would like you both to come down to see us for a day as soon as you can.'

'We will, I promise,' Pam replied. 'And we're very happy, Mrs Yates. We do love each other, and we didn't do this to hurt anyone.'

'Pam, you're a member of our family now, and we love you too, but you both need to learn that being honest and open about things is the only way to live. I'm disappointed that you didn't trust us enough to believe we would allow you to make your own decisions. You can't start a relationship with an attitude of mistrust. Please remember that in your marriage, too.'

When she came off the phone, Pam sat still for several minutes. What Bill's mother had said had hit a sensitive spot. She knew they had been deceitful to their parents, and she knew she had been deceiving Bill. It had gone on so long now she was wondering how he would react when he finally knew the whole truth. When Bill came home, she told him about his mother's call. He looked very upset. Then he said, 'I don't blame her for being hurt and angry. I know I have been lying to them since we got married. I'd better call her and at least let her know I'm sorry.'

'I'm sorry, Bill,' Pam said honestly. 'I suppose I'm the one at fault. You wanted to call her, and I talked you out of it. I was afraid she would convince you not to get married.'

'No. I'm the one at fault. I know I'm supposed to be the leader in our home. If I had had the courage I would have been honest with my parents from the beginning. I just hope this doesn't affect our relationship with them from now on.'

After a brief conversation with his mother and father, Bill hung up the phone. 'Well, they're both hurt,' he said. 'But they both want you to know they're glad to have you as a member of our family, and they will make the best of the situation. My dad said that we will have to be financially independent in the future, as he believes that now we are married we should stand on our own feet.' They're going to give us £500 as a wedding gift to get us started. Of course, we will have to repay our student loans, but we knew that from the start.'

Pam decided she would wait to tell Bill about the other debts until he had a chance to recover from the shock of telling his parents. The opportunity didn't arise before graduation, and with the £500 from Bill's parents they were able to get by for the next month.

Bill got a job in a music shop. Although it didn't pay much, he thought he would be able to get something better after the summer break when all the other students went back to college. One evening he answered the doorbell and there stood Pam's mother. 'Mrs Carlisle, come in.'

'Bill, I need to talk to you and Pam about something urgently. Is she here?'

'Yes, she is,' he replied.

At that moment Pam came through from the bedroom saying, 'Who's at the door?' When she saw her mother she looked rather worried. 'Mum, what are you doing here?' she asked in a hollow voice.

'You know very well what I'm doing here,' her mother answered. 'It's about these.' With that she thrust a handful of credit card receipts in front of her. 'You told me you were going to take care of these, and now I have received notice that they are going to sue me.'

'What are these?' Bill asked as Pam made her way to the sofa.

'They're bills run up on my credit card,' Pam's mother said in an accusing tone. 'Didn't Pam tell you I called her about them nearly two months ago?'

Bill looked over at Pam. One glance told him the answer. 'No, she didn't,' he said. 'But if they're our bills, I give you my word we'll pay every one of them, Mrs Carlisle.'

'Well, I hope you will,' she replied as she headed for the door again. 'I want you both to know how disappointed I am that you started out this way. It's partly my fault, too. Apparently we didn't teach Pam some things she needed to know, especially about handling money. We always lived within our means and we always assumed our daughter would know how to do the same.' With that she walked over to Pam, who was crying, and hugged her.

'I love you, Pam, but you need to grow up. When you take on the rights of an adult, you also take on the responsibilities. I can't pay these bills, but I wouldn't even if I could. You need to accept the consequences of your actions. And you need to be totally honest with your husband,' she said in a solemn tone.

After Pam's mother left, Bill sat down to talk to Pam about the bills. 'How much do we really owe, Pam?' he asked with as much control as possible.

'I don't know,' she replied. 'I haven't added up all the bills yet. I'm sorry for not telling you before. I didn't want to bother you during your finals and then I was afraid to tell you.'

'You don't need to be afraid to tell me anything. But we do need to work out exactly how much we owe and how we're going to pay.'

After two hours of poring over the bills that had come in, and estimating those which had not yet been sent, Bill came up with a figure of nearly £3,000.

'What are we going to do?' Pam asked.

'I don't know right now,' he answered. 'But studying for my PhD is out for the time being and I need to look for a better job, or we'll get into an even worse mess.'

'I can get a job, too,' Pam offered. 'School doesn't start again for nearly three months, so I won't know about a teaching job for a month or more.'

'Pam, we're both going to have to make some sacrifices to pay these debts. I've been really foolish not to see that we were living beyond our means – I suppose I just didn't want to know. I'm going to see Pastor Riggs tomorrow to see if he knows anyone who can help us sort this out.'

The next day Bill called in to see the minister and told him what had happened. 'Unfortunately, Bill, what has happened to you and Pam is not unusual today. Too much credit is put in the hands of young people who have little or no idea how to control the use of it. I'm sure Pam was as shocked as her mother to find out how much she had spent.'

'There's no question about that,' Bill replied. 'But what I need to know is what we can do about it. We'll pay back everything in time, but right now it looks pretty hopeless.'

'It's never hopeless if you're willing to admit your mistakes and correct them,' Pastor Riggs commented. 'I want you to call one of our elders who is a debt counsellor and he will arrange to meet you and Pam.'

Bill immediately called Chris Wilson, the elder Pastor

Riggs referred him to. 'I can see you and Pam this evening. I'll meet you at the church office at seven o'clock if that's OK with you.'

'That will be fine,' Bill said. 'And thank you for seeing us so quickly.'

At 7.00 pm Bill and Pam were waiting outside the church office. Chris Wilson arrived and Bill recognised him from a meeting he had attended more than a year ago. He had spoken on the need to be good managers of the material things God has provided. 'I really wish I had listened better,' Bill thought to himself.

Bill and Pam described the events of the past few months that had brought them to their present situation. Chris Wilson made several notes as they discussed the particular events. 'As I see it,' he said, 'you have several symptoms and two basic problems.'

'What do you mean?' Pam asked. 'What's the difference?'

'The problems created the symptoms,' he replied. 'For instance, you now owe nearly £3,000 in consumer debt. But I believe that's a symptom of a much deeper problem. If your parents just gave you the money to pay off your debts, I think they would be doing you a disservice because it's likely that you would repeat the same mistakes again.'

'Not me,' Pam said emphatically.

'I know that's what you think right now, Pam,' he said. 'And probably you wouldn't repeat exactly the same mistakes. But indulgence comes in many forms, and future mistakes can create much more severe consequences. I've seen people who earn more than £100,000 a year get deeply into debt because their impulses grew even faster than their salaries.

'I think I can help you overcome your present circumstances if you're willing to sacrifice for a while. But unless you recognise the problems and solve them, you'll be back again,'

'What do you think our problems are?' Bill asked.

'As I see it, Bill, your problem stems from a lack of self-confidence. But it shows itself in the fact that you haven't accepted your role as the head of your family.'

'What do you mean?'

'First, you allowed yourself to be led into a quick marriage and because you didn't want to hurt Pam's feelings, you weren't honest with her. No sound relationship can ever be built on a foundation of fear. Remember what the Bible teaches – perfect love casts out all fear.'

'But I don't want to dictate to Pam,' Bill argued. But even as he said it, he knew somewhere deep inside that what Chris Wilson said was right. He did fear losing Pam, and that was his prime motivation for getting married so quickly. He had seen the foolishness of what they were doing even from the beginning, but he didn't have the courage to tell her no.

'I don't mean that you should dictate to your wife, Bill. She is to be your partner. But you must accept that God's plan for the husband is to be the head of the family and lead them. Pam has a stronger personality and will tend to set the pace.'

'But I don't want to boss Bill around,' Pam protested. 'I want to be a good wife and a friend.'

'And I believe you do, Pam, or I wouldn't have brought this up so bluntly on our first visit. But you need to realise that you have a more dominant personality and that you must learn to control it.'

'Is that the second problem then?' she asked.

'No, the second problem you need to deal with is your indulgent attitude,' Chris Wilson said bluntly.

'What!' Pam said. 'I don't think I have an indulgent attitude. I've never wasted money before this.'

'But Pam, you never had the opportunity before,' Chris Wilson said. 'From what you said I suspect that your dad ran your home and doled out the money he wanted you to have. And he was probably pretty cautious with his money, wasn't he?'

'Well, yes,' Pam agreed. 'I never thought about having an indulgent attitude.'

'Some of the spending was ignorance about credit cards. But when the total comes to nearly £3,000 it usually goes far beyond just simple ignorance. Some people have such an indulgent attitude that they cannot resist anything they don't already have. It is almost an obsession. Often it's not even for themselves. They will even buy gifts for other people using their credit cards.'

Pam thought about the watch she had bought for Bill. He had protested, but she'd convinced him to keep it.

Chris Wilson continued, 'We all like to buy things. And we can all indulge, given the opportunity and the resources. But some people are what I would call shop-a-holics. They feel good when they're buying something, even if they know they can't afford it.'

Pam realised that much of what had been said applied to her. She never had splurged very much, but she hadn't had the opportunity until she had her mother's credit card. Then it became a need she had to satisfy. She had felt the same way about getting married that weekend. She didn't think she was going to lose Bill, but she wasn't willing to take the chance. 'Does that mean I should never handle the money again?' Pam asked dejectedly.

'Not at all. It just means that you need to realise that Bill is in your life to offset your imbalances, just as you are to offset his. When you recognise what those imbalances are and learn to communicate about them openly, you'll be further along than ninety per cent of couples today. I'll give you some homework to do together to help you to understand God's plan for your marriage and your finances. In the meantime, we need to deal with the immediate problem – these debts. I notice in your list of assets you have a stereo and television. Anything else of any substantial value, like an insurance policy or shares?'

'No,' Bill replied, 'just the normal junk furniture that students accumulate.'

'Actually, I do have a small insurance policy that Dad set

up for me when I was a little girl,' Pam said.

'Do you know if it has any cash value?' Chris Wilson asked.

'I think so. I had forgotten that I even had it until you mentioned insurance. Dad said it would pay a lump sum but I don't know how much.'

'OK, what we have to work with then is the potential sale of a stereo and TV, and some cash in an insurance policy. This isn't going to be easy, but it is possible for you to clear your debts. You both need to be totally realistic about your situation, and since we don't have a lot of leeway in time, I'm going to set it out for you. I hope this doesn't frighten you off, but you need to face reality.

'First, the credit card company has already started action against Pam's mother. In less than two weeks there will be a hearing and I feel sure the court will grant the petition to allow bailiffs to take some of her property unless we can work out another arrangement in the meantime. Secondly, even without the debts, you're living beyond your means. Thirdly, I assume that the stereo and TV were bought with the credit card, so you need to sell them. Obviously, you won't get back what you paid, but that's the way it is.

'Even so, your budget won't balance while you're paying off the remaining debts unless you both work. That means you have another choice to make. Pam, you will have to find a job as soon as possible, and Bill, you'll have to find another job with a more stable income.'

'We've already decided to do that,' Bill offered. 'And I realise that I won't be able to start my PhD next year.'

'Not necessarily. If you could live with one set of parents and go to college closer to home, it might be possible to fit in some study time.'

'I don't know about that,' Bill said. 'I think both our parents are pretty fed up with us at the moment.'

'Do you really blame them?' Chris Wilson said. 'So far you have got married on impulse, failed to tell the people who love you the most, charged £3,000 to someone else's credit card, and have a credit card company ready to sue your mother.'

'I suppose when you look at it that way, we do look a little immature, don't we?' Pam said.

'To say the least. Now it's time to start doing things God's way.'

'What do you mean?' Bill asked.

'Principle number one is to sell whatever you don't actually need to live on and give the money to your creditors. Proverbs 3:27-28 says, 'Do not withhold good from those who deserve it, when it is in your power to act. Do not say to your neighbour, "Come back later; I'll give it tomorrow" – when you now have it with you.'

'Principle number two is to go to your creditors and be open and honest with them. Then work out a repayment plan with them. Matthew 5:25 says, 'Settle matters quickly with your adversary who is taking you to court. Do it while you are still with him on the way, or he may hand you over to the judge, and the judge may hand you over to the officer, and you may be thrown into prison.

'And the last principle you need to apply is to think and plan before you act. Luke 14:28-29 says, "Suppose one of you wants to build a tower. Will he not first sit down and estimate the cost to see if he has enough money to complete it? For if he lays the foundation and is not able to finish it, everyone who sees it will ridicule him, saying, 'This fellow began to build and was not able to finish'."

'From now on you both need to promise that you won't make impetuous decisions and that you will pray about every decision and discuss it thoroughly.

'Pam, you have been blessed with an ability to lead and direct. Those qualities will be very beneficial both in your career and in the home. But you must be willing to listen and follow Bill's direction. God promises to guide your decisions, but only if you operate as a team.

'Now I'd like you both to contact the bank and the credit card company and work out a repayment plan. Tell them you are in the process of selling some assets and will pay them that money as soon as you have it. Feel free to tell them you're working with me. They can call me for verification. And one more thing. I will do everything I can to help you get out of this situation, but you must agree to develop a budget together and stick to it during this process. If not, I would be better off spending my time with people who are willing to listen.'

'I promise we'll stick to the plan. I want to get out of this mess and get our lives back on track,' Bill said.

'And what about you, Pam?' Mr Wilson asked.

'I want to get out of this mess, naturally,' Pam replied. 'But I am really afraid that what you said about my being an impulse spender is true. What if I can't control myself and do this again?'

'Pam, spending is not like alcoholism or drug addiction, although it can be if you don't exercise self-control. You need to establish some guidelines for yourself that include relying on Bill to balance your extremes. Once you make a budget, don't break it. That doesn't mean you can't ever spend any money, or that you won't need some free money for your own use. Everybody does. But limit yourself to what you can afford, and don't rely on credit cards to fill in the gaps. Credit makes it too easy to overspend and is too difficult to pay back. If you stick to your repayment plan, you'll be out of debt in a short while, perhaps even a few months. But if you don't, you may well find yourselves as one of those unfortunate statistics of divorce. Nearly half of all new marriages fail, many of them Christian. And the vast majority claim that financial problems caused their marital problems.'

'I can believe that,' Bill said. 'I don't know what we would have done if it weren't for you, I was really beginning to feel the pressure.'

'I haven't done anything but help you realise that there is

an answer to your problems. Now it's up to you to work out the details and stick to them. I'll give you some materials that will help you understand the basic principles from God's word. These must be your guide if you want to make good decisions in the future. You need to learn how to balance a cheque book accurately and how to organise a monthly budget. We'll work that out together over the next few weeks.'

They sold the stereo and television for £600, which they put towards paying off the loan, and the cash from the insurance policy reduced the debt by another £700. Bill took a job with a national delivery service that paid nearly twice what he had been making, and Pam got a job in telephone sales. Between the two of them they were able to pay off the debt in six months, although it took a lot of scrimping.

In the autumn Pam accepted a teaching position and they began to settle into a reasonably normal routine. Over the course of three months they met with Chris Wilson once a week. During that time they learned how to balance and maintain their bank account and how to develop a realistic budget. In the fourth month Chris Wilson asked them if they would be willing to counsel another young couple. Bill asked Pam, who wholeheartedly agreed, and they began their first one-to-one counselling to help another couple.

Bill ultimately went on to get his PhD in music and got a job at the university where he and Pam met. They lived with Pam's mother for about a year and a half, during which time they helped her to get started on a budget. During that time she also began training for a new career in nursing, which she was able to do as a result of their financial assistance.

Bill and Pam's financial recovery was possible only because they faced their problems honestly and worked through them together.

CHAPTER 13

THREE MAJOR EXPENSES THAT LEAD TO DEBT

As our look at three couples has demonstrated, a common thread in most of their experiences was the lack of thorough planning. Sometimes this flaw is amplified by ignorance or indulgence, but without some kind of financial plan (budget) most couples won't realise they have a problem until it overwhelms them.

Many couples think they live on a budget because they write down their cheques and balance their bank account. This is not a budget. A budget balances income and expenses and reports on the status of those each month. (To learn how to budget see Chapter Nineteen 'Debt Free Living – Check List' at the end of the book.)

There are three common ways many people get into debt:

1. The purchase of a home

Nearly every young couple in Britain dreams of owning their own home. The term 'owning' is used loosely here because what that means for most couples is paying a mortgage. So the common definition of owning is 'as opposed to renting'. Many couples try to buy a home too soon, or pay too much and end up in financial trouble. Unfortunately, quite often they don't realise that owning the home created their financial troubles because it took too large a portion of their spendable income. Just as with Paul and Julie, the first couple discussed in this book, they find themselves sinking further behind every month.

The percentage of an average family's budget that should be spent on a mortgage is no more that twenty-five per cent of net spendable income (after tithes and taxes). Add to the mortgage payments the cost of utilities, insurance, maintenance and incidentals, and the percentage climbs to around thirty-five per cent. Unfortunately, many couples commit more than sixty per cent of their budget to housing. There is virtually no way to handle that kind of cost. If they plan out their spending as a whole for the year, the strain would be apparent. But because they usually look only at one month they don't see it. The monthly budget couples typically work out does not take into account clothes, car repairs, and other major expenses such as insurance. So it is unrealistic.

If you can afford to purchase a home within your budget, that makes sense. But if you wreck your budget just to get into a home, that makes no sense at all. The compulsion we have for buying large, expensive homes is just a reflection of poor stewardship in general. Most couples would be far better off saving for a down payment of at least twenty per cent and buying a smaller, less expensive home initially. Certainly the purchase of a home for a young couple should never be determined on the basis of their combined incomes, for if one income fails (for example, if the wife becomes pregnant and she has to stay at home to look after the child) the entire purchase will be in jeopardy. This violates the principle of good planning according to Proverbs 22:3, 'A prudent man sees danger and takes refuge, but the simple keep going and suffer for it.'

Too often Christians limit their faith in God only to the unseen things such as salvation and good health. But we happen to believe that God manifests himself in material ways to those who trust him. Let us make it very clear that we are not talking about a health and prosperity gospel. As Job said earlier, and the apostle Paul reiterated in Romans 11:34-35, 'Who has known the mind of the Lord? Or who has been his counsellor? Who has ever given to God, that God should repay him?' The decision to help individuals with their finances is the Lord's. But we do believe God wants to support strongly those who love and trust him, just as a parent does a loving and obedient child. After all, that is what the Lord told us in Matthew 7:11, 'If you, then, though you are evil, know how to give good gifts to your children, how much more will your Father in heaven give good gifts to those who ask him.'

Andy and Diane did what most young couples do within the first five years of their marriage: they bought a home based on two incomes, and even then it stretched their budget. Diane got pregnant and was unable to work regularly, so they fell steadily behind with their bills. Within a few months she was juggling payments based on which creditor was threatening legal action. The stress on Diane threatened her pregnancy and made her even more miserable. The doctor feared she might lose the baby and ordered her to bed for complete rest. But the problems didn't ease – they intensified because of the greater financial drain.

Andy found himself resentful of the fact that Diane couldn't work, and often they would end the evening sleeping in separate rooms in the 'dream house'. Andy also found himself using his credit card to buy petrol and other basic necessities because he was so low on cash. As a result of a seminar they attended at their church they recognised a need for help.

The home they had bought consumed nearly seventy per cent of Andy's take-home pay. It was obvious that it was totally beyond their financial ability. When this was pointed out, Diane became very defensive. She was not willing to discuss the prospect of selling their home and Andy was extremely uncomfortable even talking about it. Diane had grown up as a minister's daughter, and when her father was killed in a car accident, her mother had to leave the manse within three months. They were left homeless and nearly destitute for several years. That experience had left such an impression on Diane that she almost had a paranoia about selling her home.

The couple left the appointment with the debt counsellor with the details of how to establish a budget that would allocate something for every category of spending. In addition they were asked to determine how much they could cut back to begin repaying some of the existing debt.

When they returned in two weeks the answer was clear. When the mortgage had been paid there was nothing left over to pay other bills. In fact, the true monthly deficit was close to £300. They had tried to discuss the issue of the home, but it always ended with Diane crying, so Andy avoided the subject entirely. They were both committed Christians and wanted to do what was right, but were stumped by something as material as a house.

Diane was asked if she really believed she could trust God. She said she did, but it was clear she had great difficulty with the idea of giving up her home. She was intelligent and realised that the home was beyond their means at that time – but as with any other paranoia, if it made sense it wouldn't have been a paranoia. It was clear that no one was going to talk her into voluntarily selling her home. She dug in her heels. Although selling their home might be the best thing for her, she couldn't see it that way at all.

The one thing that Diane did agree with was the fact that the house was too expensive for their budget, and that month by month the situation would get worse if they didn't do something. At that point the decision had to be Diane's. Either she would trust God in the matter of her home or she wouldn't. A few weeks later she called tearfully to report that their financial situation had deteriorated. Andy had made a commitment not to use the credit cards and had actually cut them up. Shortly after he did so the car broke down. Having no money for repairs, he decided he would have to leave the car in the garage and try and get a lift to work. Members of their house group heard about this and gave them a gift to get the car repaired.

Their actions had a great impact on Diane. Until that time she had been thinking that God only worked through supernatural miracles. She had prayed for everything from a total restoration of their car, to asking God for someone to give them a new one. But she never even considered the simple alternative that those with a surplus might give a little to help get their old one running again. She also realised that even though she hated to see Andy having to accept a lift to work every day, she had still regarded any discussions about the house as off limits. The house had become her idol.

When they went to their next session with the counsellor, Diane had already put the house up for sale and had had a tentative offer. She wasn't jubilant about the decision, but she was resolved. She was determined that nothing would make her take her eyes off the Lord again.

Several weeks later their home was sold, and the equity from the sale cleared all the bills. They moved into a two-bedroom flat and within three months they had led their new neighbours to the Lord. Diane decided that was obviously why the Lord had moved them out of their home – to meet that greater need. But she was able to learn a lesson that most Christians miss because they never really surrender the material areas of their lives to the Lord.

Almost a year after they had sold their home, a member of their church called them. He was moving to America for several years and wanted to keep the home he lived in because it had been his family home for several generations; but he didn't want to leave it vacant. The company he worked for was willing to pay all his costs, so he didn't have a financial need to rent it. In fact, he was willing to pay the costs of a house-sitter.

He asked Andy and Diane if they would be willing to live in his house for five years – all expenses paid and a salary of £200 a month. They jumped at the chance and solved their housing problems in a single stroke.

They could have stayed in their home until they were evicted, or until Diane went back to work after the baby was born. Then they probably could have limped along until the next crisis hit. Instead they chose to trust God and discover what was his plan for their lives. He'll work with anyone who's available and willing to trust him.

2. Car purchases

The second most common source of debt is the purchase of a new car. Quite often a couple who can't afford to buy a new home decide on a new car as a compromise. Unfortunately, it's not a good compromise because cars now sell for prices that houses sold for twenty years ago. This is the major debt trap for most singles who overspend.

Most young people are so prone to buying on credit that they don't even ask the price of the car – just how much the monthly payments are. The car industry understands this mentality well. When they want to stimulate sales for a product that has been inflated out of proportion to most other consumer products, they advertise low interest rates as the biggest selling feature. Usually that is the deciding factor for a generation that has been raised on new cars and nice houses. To the young couple already in debt because of a home that is too expensive, a new car appears to be the answer to their car problems. So they trade in the old car that cost them £75 a month to keep running, for a new car with £150 monthly payments. But it's not good economics as they will discover a couple of months down the line.

A family seeking to sell an almost new car to relieve debt is usually shocked to discover how little it's worth on the open market. If it is sold at auction, which is often the case when a car is repossessed, the sale price may be half of what an identical car sells for at a garage. Typically, when a car is repossessed for failure to make the payments, the car is sold at a loss, and the finance company sues the borrower for the difference.

The same is true of a leased car. The lease contract to pay is just as binding as a purchase agreement. If the leasing company has to repossess a leased car, it rarely will attempt to re-lease it. The typical leasee wants a brand-new car, not a used one. The leased car is auctioned off, and the leasee is sued for the deficiency.

Buying new cars has placed a bondage on many couples. However, if someone has his or her finances under control and can save for the cost of a new car, it is his or her decision whether or not to buy one. One person may think a new car is a bad buy, while another may think it represents better value. But the one thing neither of them can disagree about is that when you borrow money to buy a car you are going to become liable for the loan.

3. Scheduled disasters

Do you know how to schedule a financial disaster? It is simple. Fail to plan for predictable expenses that haven't come due yet. A common example of this is failing to plan for predictable car maintenance. Cars have a regular cycle of problems. About every twenty-five to thirty thousand miles they need tyres, fan belts, spark plugs, and so on. Once this is acknowledged, the sensible thing to do is to anticipate those expenses and budget for them. Failure to plan in this way is a major reason many people end up in debt. When the expenses occur they must be paid, so the only alternative available is often a credit card.

Why do intelligent people fail to anticipate known expenses? Because when they try to work them into their spending plan (a budget) they don't fit. So they simply ignore those expenses until a crisis arrives. To do otherwise would require adjustments in the other areas of spending, such as housing, cars and holidays. This is the head in the sand syndrome.

It is common to see this problem when one counsels engaged couples about their first year's budget. When asked if they have developed a budget, usually they respond, 'Yes, we have and everything worked out fine.' But when their budget is reviewed, it reveals that they have made no provision for clothes, insurance, car repairs or holidays.

One young couple thought they had worked out a way to beat the system. They had financial problems that resulted from all of the above symptoms. In other words, they had a home that was too expensive, two cars and a variety of consumer debts from department stores. There was absolutely no way their income could ever stretch far enough to manage their expenses, so they charged nearly everything each month to their credit cards, except their utilities. They had been able to do that for nearly three years without being behind on a single monthly minimum payment. Their method was to charge on one card until the limit was reached, and then pay that card off with two or three others. Being good credit customers they had no trouble getting their credit limits raised, so on they went for the best part of three years. Ultimately, the whole house of credit came tumbling down because it became too large to manage. When their credit binge ended they owed nearly £23,000 in credit card debts. They were advised to go bankrupt and were considering doing so until they received notice that two of the credit card issuers were considering filing fraud charges against them. (Debts caused by fraud are not eliminated by bankruptcy and are still owed when you are eventually discharged from bankruptcy). The potential consequences of that forced them to face reality and make a commitment to repay the loans. They are still paying £500 in monthly payments – eight years later.

CHAPTER 14

UNDERSTANDING CREDIT

Since we are discussing the subject of debt in this book, we also need to discuss credit. Credit and debt are not synonymous terms, although they are used interchangeably in our society. Credit can best be defined as the establishment of a mutual trust relationship between a lender and a borrower, which can be the loan of something other than money. For instance, if I lend my lawn mower to a neighbour in exchange for the use of his caravan, we have a credit relationship. I have extended credit (the use of my lawn mower) and he is indebted to me until I use his caravan. This is called a barter exchange and is commonly done in business.

Debt, as defined previously, is a condition that exists when a loan commitment is not met, or inadequate collateral is pledged to unconditionally satisfy a loan agreement. There are two important issues in the topic of credit: how to get it and how to lose it.

How to get credit

Many people get into trouble with credit because they are desperate to get it and because it is easy for them to qualify for more than they can manage. The very best way to get credit initially is to borrow against an acceptable asset. For example, if you have saved £1,000 and want to borrow the same amount, almost any bank will lend you £1,000 using the savings as collateral. Usually the lender will charge around five per cent more for the loan than the prevailing savings rate. Then, by using the bank as a credit reference, almost anyone can qualify for a major credit card, although the credit limit would normally be the minimum amount. We don't mean to imply that everyone should get a credit card, or that everyone will be able to manage one properly. But credit is relatively simple to establish once you have opened a bank account.

It has been our experience that if someone who has never had credit wishes to acquire a credit card and tries enough places, somebody will issue him with one. The difficulty with this method is that once the first company issues a card and the person uses it wisely, other companies will soon follow suit, and he will be swamped with credit card applications. The temptation of too much credit is often overwhelming and a person can soon find himself or herself deeply in debt. We would offer the following advice to anyone using credit cards for the first time or who has ever got into trouble through the misuse of credit cards. It is good advice, and it will save you many problems.

Never use a credit card to buy anything that is not in your budget for the month (which means, of course, you will need a budget)

It is tempting to use a credit card when you are on holiday and you have run out of your allocated funds, or when you need clothes but don't have the money to take advantage of the sale bargains on offer, or when you need tyres for the car but don't have the money saved, or when you're out of work and need food, utilities and rent. But when you use a credit card as a buffer in place of trusting God, you may fall into a trap that will take you a long time to dig yourself out of.

Pay the entire credit card bill each month.

Many people say they never misuse their credit cards because they pay them completely each month. Using credit cards – or any credit – wisely is not just a matter of being able to pay them off on time. Credit cards are the number one tool for impulse buying in our society. And impulse buying is generally the prerequisite for indulgent buying. Simply put, consumers will buy things they don't need and pay more for them when using credit. Credit is less personal than cash in your pocket, and people tend to use it more carelessly.

If you don't pay the credit card charges every month you will pay a usurious rate of interest and paying that represents poor stewardship. In addition, by accumulating credit card charges you run the risk of *debt*.

The first time you find yourself unable to pay the total charges, destroy the cards.

The problem is not the use of credit. It is the misuse of credit.

Credit to avoid

There are some sources of credit that are simply bad deals even by today's standards. In the constant drive to create more ways for couples to borrow money, many lenders have stepped over the borderline of common sense, in our opinion. But it is the responsibility of the borrower to avoid the use of credit that encourages poor stewardship. The following are a few examples of credit sources to avoid.

Bank overdrafts

Most banks today offer what is called an authorised overdraft. Thus when a customer writes a cheque in excess of what he or she has in the bank, the cheque will be honoured (paid by the bank). Sounds like a good deal, doesn't it? After all, if you write a cheque beyond your balance, you don't want it to 'bounce' do you? There would be penalties for the returned cheque and possible charges from the merchant as well. So why not take the authorised overdraft?

Many people who had taken an automatic overdraft have got into debt because of it. The people who regularly go overdrawn are those who don't know their cheque book balance. Obviously there are those who are dishonest and purposely go overdrawn, but they are a minority and usually can't get an authorised overdraft anyway.

An authorised overdraft is an enticement for couples to avoid balancing their bank accounts. Authorised overdrafts are not a benevolent act on the part of the bank. Those accounts accumulate interest from the date of transaction, not after the normal thirty days common to credit card accounts.

Finance company loans

We don't want to impugn the integrity of all finance companies, because there are many honest and ethical companies in business. But some finance companies use high pressure tactics in their operation and charge very high interest. Finance companies specialise in lending to those who can't qualify for loans through normal channels such as banks, building societies or credit cards. They often specialise in high pressure tactics to collect their money if necessary. If you are being pursued by one of these companies, you need to take advice quickly.

Second mortgages

Some people might wonder why we place second mortgages in this section about credit to avoid. In general these loans have several features that make them hazardous to an individual's long-term financial health. First, they encourage someone to borrow against the equity in their home, when in truth they should be working to pay the remaining mortgage off. Secondly, the interest rates are usually variable, meaning that they can be adjusted as the prevailing interest rates change. That puts the borrower in a position in which it is nearly impossible to control future costs. Thirdly, in many cases it will be they who instigate repossession proceedings if you should fall into arrears, rather than your main mortgage company, particularly if house prices are falling.

Taxes

If there is one source of credit you should diligently avoid, it is the Inland Revenue – or to put it another way, don't live on money that you owe to the tax man. Many couples are tempted to do this, especially couples who are self-employed. Once the tax man catches up, however, they can be very hard to negotiate with and will often resist calls for renegotiation that other creditors might agree to.

How to determine the 'real' interest rate

In conclusion to this discussion on credit, it is vital that you understand how to determine the true interest rate someone is quoting you. The Consumer Credit Act now requires that all interest be stated in Annualised Percentage Rate (APR). That establishes one standard for all interest charged, regardless of how it is calculated. Let us present an example. If you borrowed £100 for one year and at the end of twelve months repaid £110 you had an APR of ten per cent. But suppose you borrowed £100 and made a monthly payment of £9.17. At the end of one year you will have repaid £110 but the Annualised Percentage Rate would have been higher. Why? Because you didn't actually have use of the entire £100 for the whole year, the APR was closer to twelve per cent.

Additionally, the Consumer Credit Act requires that all finances charged be clearly shown before you sign an instalment contract. Many times service fees, and extra charges can substantially increase the cost of a loan. A lender who fails to reveal all the costs risks penalties and forfeiture of all accumulated interest. If you believe you have been the victim of unfair lending, you need to contact the Office of Fair Trading.

In the final analysis, the best protection you can have against the misuse of credit is to determine that you will control the use of credit and refuse to allow it to control you. As stated earlier, there is no substitute for personal discipline and self-control in the area of credit.

By now we trust that you understand that the misuse of credit – not credit itself – is the problem. The Bible does not teach that you can never borrow. It teaches that borrowing is hazardous if done unwisely. Every Christian should have a goal to be debt-free eventually. If you can't be debt-free right now, set a goal and work towards it.

CHAPTER 15

DEBT CONSOLIDATION LOANS

When John and Heather came into the counsellor's office they were obviously stressed. They were nervous about being there and embarrassed to tell their story. John was a solicitor with a firm specialising in property deals. John appeared to be the epitome of success. He was rising fast in his firm because of his quick mind and hard work. He and Heather had just bought a home in *the* area of town and were expecting their first child. Their situation looked good when viewed from the outside. Inside, however, it was a different matter.

Within the last two years John's salary and bonus had increased from £25,000 a year to nearly £34,000 and the future prospects looked even better. They felt they could afford a better home and had decided to take the plunge and buy in the area where other, older members of the firm lived. The new home cost £180,000 and their mortgage repayments were over £1,000 a month after a down payment of £20,000. They lacked the funds for the total down payment, but John arranged an £18,000 advance on his bonus towards the deposit. When they moved Heather bought curtains, carpets and wallpaper all with John's encouragement. He said (and believed) that what they were doing was in the best interest of his career. Before they finished decorating and paying for moving costs, their bills totalled nearly £11,000.

By this time Heather was beginning to feel a little nervous about their spending, particularly since they didn't have the money to pay for all their expenses. John told her not to worry because the sale of their first home would net enough to pay back the advance and the cost of the improvements to the new home. Indeed, they did have a contract on their first home that would net them nearly £29,000. They had a buyer who was waiting to sell his home, but who was certain it would sell quickly. So they went ahead and bought the new house, along with all the trappings, with the help of a bridging loan from the bank, based on the contingent sale of their old home which was dependent upon the sale of the buyer's home (a lot of ifs!). It's obvious that no one had ever explained to them the principle taught in Proverbs 27:1, 'Do not boast about tomorrow, for you do not know what a day may bring forth.'

As you have probably guessed, the sale of the buyer's home fell through, so he backed out of the sale on John and Heather's home. They were already in a new home with payments of more that £1,000 a month, with £11,000 of new bills – and they were continuing payments on their old home of £700 a month as well. To say the least, Heather was uneasy about their situation. Each month they fell further behind and still their house didn't sell. She begged John to drop the price, but he refused, stating that it was worth what they were asking.

Finally, after six months, they had an offer on the house, though it was £5,000 less than the original asking price. By that time John was ready to sell as he faced a higher mountain of unpaid bills each month. They netted £18,000 after paying off the outstanding bills. Virtually all of the remaining proceeds from the house went to repay the firm. In the meantime they had accumulated another £3,500 of debts from miscellaneous sources.

John finally realised that their monthly obligations were beyond his income. So he approached the bank and asked about consolidating all their outstanding debts in one loan. By that point he needed about £20,000 to consolidate everything.

The bank thought he would be a good risk, but he lacked adequate security for a loan of that size. After a great deal of negotiating they were able to take out a second mortgage on their home and assigned that year's bonus as extra security.

The first year everything went fine, or so it seemed. John earned a bonus of £15,000, bringing his earned income to nearly £40,000. He paid £5,000 towards the loan and paid nearly £6,000 in taxes on the bonus. With the rest he and Heather went to the West Indies during the winter.

Heather didn't really have a clear idea of how they were doing month by month, but she began to see final demands coming from the bank and from credit card companies. Finally she asked John to sit down and tell her exactly where they were financially. He confessed that he didn't really know. 'It just seems like there is never enough money to pay everything we owe,' he said. He agreed with Heather that they needed to do something about their budget. But then he got busy on a new project and they never got around to it.

As the final demands became more frequent, Heather began to complain to John that he had to get some help in handling their situation. He agreed, but never took the time to look for the help he needed. Finally, one afternoon, the whole situation came to a head when the bank manager called John at his office. 'I need to see you right away. Can you come in and see me this afternoon?' he asked.

'I'm really very busy today,' John replied as he looked over the contracts on his desk. He had been getting less and less productive as the pressures at home built up. It seemed that Heather was always annoyed about one thing or another.

'I must see you right away. We have been reviewing your loan and you are so far behind with the payments we will have to commence repossession proceedings.'

John felt a cold wave of fear come over him. 'You can't do that,' John pleaded. 'It would ruin me with the firm.'

'Come over and we'll discuss it. Maybe there is some solution.'

John put the phone down, his hand shaking. He knew he had financial problems, but until that moment he hadn't realised how bad they were. He was three months behind on his first mortgage and four months behind on the second. He had been promising the bank that he would catch up on the payment when his mid-year bonus came. But that bonus had been just £4,000 and it had been used to cover living expenses. John's boss had called him in to review his work over the past six months because his productivity had dropped off severely. He knew that the bank's repossessing his home might cost him his job, and he was only a year away from being made a full partner in the firm. His salary and bonuses would increase substantially then. He felt panic rising inside him as he realised that not only might he not get a partnership, he might even be released from the firm.

He left the office, telling the receptionist that he would be back in an hour or so. He went to the bank and asked if he could see Mr Barnes.

'Please sit down,' Mr Barnes said politely. He closed the door to his office. 'It would appear that you have some pretty severe financial problems,' he said.

'Well, we do have some temporary problems,' John said. 'But I'll be able to sort them out when my next bonus comes.'

'I'm afraid you need to face reality,' Mr Barnes said as he opened the file on his desk. 'I took the liberty of checking into your recent credit history. You're behind on everything, even your utility payments.'

'It seems that there just isn't enough money to cover everything each month,' John explained. 'But I'll be a partner in the firm in a few months, and my income will increase substantially then. Can't you extend the second mortgage? I would only need a few thousand pounds more to keep going until then.'

'I'm afraid I just can't do that. It's not more money you need, and another consolidation loan won't help. You're simply digging yourself a bigger pit. You're living beyond your means and using loans to make up the difference. And you'll just continue to do so, no matter how much you make. I did you a disservice by giving you the first consolidation loan on your house. You're worse off now than you were then.'

John slumped down in his chair. He wanted to argue with the bank manager but he knew that he was telling the truth. They were worse off now and there seemed to be no end to the flood of money going out.

'What can I do?' John asked in a subdued tone. 'If you repossess my house I may lose my job.'

'I found that one of the credit card companies is also planning legal action to collect their money. You may well be facing a county court judgement and an attachment of earnings order if they do.'

'That will definitely cost me my job,' John thought. 'Is there anything you can do to help?'

'Yes, I think so. But not by advancing you any more money. The bank wouldn't allow it even if I wanted to. I want you to go to a debt counsellor who will help you to work out a plan. We'll work with you in whatever action he decides you should take.'

So John and Heather arranged a meeting. The solution to their problems was difficult, but not complicated. The first step was to get an accurate picture of where they stood financially. They listed every debt and found that they had accumulated almost £3,000 of additional debt since the consolidation loan. Basically they were back on the same track they had been on before the loan, but with greater expenses each month because of the second mortgage. They were also behind on almost every debt, including a MasterCard bill that had not been paid for five months. Their basic household expenses, together with minimum payments on their debt, took 120 per cent of their income, including the average bonus John received.

Even before John took out the consolidation loan, their average monthly expenses consumed over ninety-five per cent of their income – without such costs as clothes and insurance. The consolidation loan allowed them to avoid the reality of a bad situation for a few more months. They were unable to give anything to their church, even though they had both been tithing since their youth. During the past several months they had stopped going to church and rarely prayed together, even though that had been their commitment since before they were married. As with most couples experiencing financial problems, they simply lacked the desire to seek the Lord together.

John made contact with the bank that issued the MasterCard and they agreed to accept a minimum payment on the account for three months while they were working out a permanent solution. They then contacted Mr Barnes and arranged for the bank to accept a three-month moratorium (no payments) on the second mortgage, provided that the first mortgage was brought up to date during the following month.

The plan was simple and direct. Both John and Heather realised that they were in over their heads financially and that they had to reduce their expenses. There were only two areas that could be cut substantially: housing and cars. The house and one car had to be sold if they were ever to balance their budget. Both decisions were difficult for them to accept until all the figures were on the table and visible. Then the facts dictated the decisions. They could stay in their home until it was repossessed, or sell it voluntarily. They could drive one new car, or lose them both. These were tough facts but easy decisions.

They had only one asset that could be converted into immediate cash to pay the bank: an insurance policy that John had owned for several years. Its surrender value was nearly £3,000, but they were able to sell it for fifteen per cent more than that. They used the proceeds to bring the first mortgage up to date.

They put the house up for sale and found a buyer almost immediately. They recovered enough from the sale to pay off the second mortgage and all but £4,000 of the credit card debts. These were paid off within the next year.

John and Heather rented a flat and worked hard to get their finances under control. They developed a realistic budget and began to give to the church each month. Later they began to teach a class in their church on the biblical principles of handling money and now have become recognised authorities on budgeting.

John became a partner in the law firm and now, ten years later, is one of the senior partners. He instituted a policy that all young solicitors joining the firm must attend a class on budgeting and agree to live on a budget for the first year. His feeling was that if he could get them to live on a budget for a year, they would live on one for ever. He tells his story to every new solicitor and proudly points out that he and Heather bought back the home they had to sell and now own it debt-free.

Is a consolidation loan always wrong?

One of the most common questions asked in counselling is, 'Should we consolidate?' So the logical question a Christian needs to ask is, 'Is it wrong to consolidate?' The answer is no, not necessarily. But there are some inherent problems that must be dealt with before a consolidation loan is advisable.

First, unless the problems that created the need for a consolidation loan are corrected, you may well find yourself worse off in the long run. For instance, if the debt was created by overspending on a monthly basis, the consolidation loan won't solve that problem. It will only delay the inevitable. Until the problem of overspending is solved, no consolidation loans should ever be considered. Otherwise a year or so later all the little bills will be back again and when they are combined with the consolidation loan, the situation will be worse.

No one should consider a consolidation loan until they have been living on a budget for six months and have learned to control their overspending. Once you know you have the overspending under control, it may make sense to substitute one large loan at a reduced interest rate for several smaller ones at higher rates.

Secondly, with a consolidation loan, there is always the tendency to stop worrying once the supposed solution has been found. Many people actually spend more the month after consolidating than they ever did before, often taking a holiday or buying a new TV or video. Why? Because they think the pressure is off and they can relax. That is a false security created by the temporary removal of financial pressure. You need to resist that urge to splurge.

Thirdly, all too often when people consolidate, they borrow more than what is needed to pay the outstanding bills. Then they buy things they have wanted for several months but were unable to afford. The purchases may actually be needed items such as a refrigerator, a washing machine, or a car.

What's wrong with that? Nothing, as long as the individual has disciplined himself and saved the money to buy those things. But for those who already have discipline problems, it's just one more way to splurge.

In our generation there are almost limitless temptations to spend. Thousands of people actually make their living thinking of new ways to lend money and collect interest. Perhaps the most common method of consolidating since the late eighties is through second mortgages. We believe second mortgages are one of the worst ideas ever pushed on the average family. They encourage them to put their homes in jeopardy and borrow to buy things they can easily do without, such as new cars.

CHAPTER 16

DEALING WITH CREDITORS

The way someone deals with his creditors says a lot about his character and about Christianity. Many times Christians complain about a creditor who is especially aggressive about wanting his money back. But although in our generation we have legally limited a lender's ability to collect his money, that does not negate his authority over the borrower.

The principle to remember is always to run towards your creditors, not away from them. When counselling, the most difficult problem to overcome is attempting to negotiate with a creditor who has been ignored for a long time. Put yourself in the position of the creditor. Wouldn't you want to know that someone was willing to pay but couldn't, rather than be left totally in the dark?

Unfortunately, many people who can't pay everything don't pay anything. That is also an error. Pay what you can each month, even if it is only a partial payment. And don't make unrealistic promises in order to get a creditor off your back. You need to approach the promise to pay with the same degree of caution that you would the signing of a contract. When you give your word, you need to keep it. If you make a promise that you know you won't be able to keep, you have violated the principle of vows. Listen to what the judge said about promises in Ecclesiastes 5:4-5, 'When you make a vow to God, do not delay in fulfilling it. He has no pleasure in fools; fulfil your vow. It is better not to vow than to make a vow and not fulfil it.'

Have a written plan

Creditors respond best to a specific request that is backed by a detailed plan in writing. Most creditors have been deceived so many times by people making promises that they have become very cynical. Almost anyone under the threat of a court summons will make the appropriate promises. Consequently most creditors have developed an immunity to tearful pleas from bad debtors. However, most will respond to a written plan backed by guaranteed action on the part of a debtor. That's why a counsellor is often necessary in dealing with belligerent creditors. A counsellor generally represents an objective third party who will enforce the agreements.

Step 1: A detailed report

You need to state in detail exactly how much you owe and what the minimum monthly requirements are.

Table 16.1
List of Debts

TO WHOM OWED	CONTACT PHONE NO. ADDRESS	PAY OFF	PAYMENTS REMAINING	MONTHLY PAYMENT	DATE

It is vital to be totally honest and as accurate as possible. That's why both partners need to be involved in drawing up a list of debts. One partner will often overlook something that the other will recall. The obvious difficulty is that if one is hiding something from the other, he or she will avoid recording it. Since financial problems are usually accompanied by other problems, it is not unusual for one partner to try to continue the deception if they are afraid to be honest. There is no way that one person alone can resolve a debt problem that affects two people.

If you are the offended party, try to control your reaction to any new revelation about your finances. Your response will often determine whether or not your partner will be honest in the future. If you are the offending party, you need to accept the risks involved with total honesty and lay all the finances out on the table (literally). Ultimately the truth will be revealed anyway and the reaction will be worse the longer it is delayed. Lying and deception are sins, and God has never said there will be no consequence of sin, but he also promised that if we confess our sin, he is faithful to forgive us (1 John 1:9).

Step 2: A budget

Once the list of creditors is complete and accurate, the next step is to develop a budget that will tell you and the creditors how much you can pay them each month.

Table 16.2 is a sample budget. The left side shows the budget based on previous spending records. The amounts on the right represent the new budget submitted to the creditors. Notice that the amount allocated for debts doesn't match the previous monthly total calculated from the creditor's chart. The only thing that can be done is to ask the creditors to accept a lesser amount for a period of time. Before that request can be made, however, we need to know how long that period will be. Often that depends on whether or not there are assets that can be sold and how long it will take to sell them. Also the option of a consolidation loan must be considered it if will satisfy all the creditors.

Table 16.2
Budget Analysis

GROSS PER YEAR £24,000   GROSS PER MONTH £2,000
NET SPENDABLE INCOME PER MONTH £1,350

Monthly Payment	Existing Budget	New Budget
1. Tithe	£200	£200
2. Taxes	£450	£450
Net Spendable Income Per Month	**£1,350**	**£1,350**
3. Mortgage	£550	£550
4. Food	£240	£230
5. Cars	£230	£120[1]
6. Insurance	£0	£95[2]
7. Debts	£160	£100[3]
8. Entertainment and Recreation	£70	£50
9. Clothing	£25	£75
10. Savings	£25	£50[4]
11. Miscellaneous	£100	£80
TOTAL (items 3 to 11)	**£1,400**	**£1,350**

1 Sold second car
2 Added life and health insurance
3 Paid off two loans with car proceeds
4 Increased the emergency fund

Obviously, creditors are not going to agree to a plan providing them with no payments if there is no promise of an appreciable change in the future. But often creditors will accept smaller payments for a period of time when there does appear to be a logical reason for the temporary reduction. If the reduced payments are within seventy-five per cent of the actual payments, there is usually no difficulty in getting the creditors to accept a reduced payment plan indefinitely. Obviously that depends on the creditor. Some are restricted by company policies. In those cases it is often necessary to appeal to higher management. In almost all cases they will require a third party to negotiate on behalf of the debtor.

Many companies have a working agreement with organisations such as the Citizens Advice Bureau or Consumer Credit Counselling Service and they can usually negotiate reduced payment schedules as well as reduced interest fees. Credit Action runs a national freephone helpline (0800 591084) which is staffed by Christian financial counsellors.

What happens when a creditor won't co-operate?

Most attempts to get out of debt sound great because you usually hear the success stories. But what happens when the creditors refuse to co-operate? The principle to remember is this: don't give up too soon. Often, when the debts are outstanding, the original lender will have already turned the account over to a collection agency. The collection agency is less likely to co-operate and more likely to sue. But unless the debt has actually been sold to a third party, the original lender can still control the proceedings.

Generally speaking, the local office of a national company has only limited ability to negotiate once a loan is badly in arrears. So your best chance of reaching an agreement is to request the name of the national arrears manager and try to work out a settlement with him. You must suggest a reasonable plan, and you will usually need a third party reference, such as a counsellor.

However, there are times when the best efforts don't work. That is usually because the debtor has made frequent promises that were not kept, or because he failed to respond to the many warnings the company sent out before pursuing legal action. The actions a creditor normally takes will fall into one of three areas.

Repossession

If you have borrowed for a specific asset such as a house, car, television, refrigerator, or furniture and the asset is security for the loan, a creditor has the right to repossess it according to the terms of your loan agreement.

Agreements give the creditor the right to repossess with written notice if the account is in arrears. Most people have heard stories of professional bailiffs who sneak into the debtor's drive and take away the car. Indeed that can happen, and if a repossession order has been granted, it is perfectly legal.

More common is for a bad debtor to receive written notice that a creditor is taking action in court. Normally there is a legal waiting period, during which you have the right to present your case, if there is a dispute. However, if a debtor ignores the notification and does not enter a defence, the judgement is automatic, and the creditor can and will repossess the assets.

We have received many an urgent phone call from a frantic homeowner whose house was about to be repossessed. Often we find out only the day before the hearing. By this stage it is often too late, unless the entire amount outstanding can be offered to the lender. If a judgement has already been handed down, it may require the entire mortgage balance. Unfortunately, the lenders usually would have worked out a reasonable plan to avoid having to repossess the home because of the expenses involved and the bad publicity that often accompanies such action, but once the legal process is started it is difficult to abort.

Armed with a court order, a creditor's representative can indeed come into a debtor's home to repossess it. If refused entry, he can simply bring the police with him the next time and order the debtor to comply. Failure to comply with the court order can result in arrest and additional expenses.

Most loan contracts contain clauses that allow the creditor to collect all costs associated with legal action or repossessions. You need to read any contract you sign very carefully because the costs of such actions can be significant.

Once the merchandise is recovered, the creditor may choose to sell it and apply the proceeds against the outstanding debt. The difference between the loan balance and the sale proceeds is called a deficiency, and the creditor has the right to bill the debtor for that amount plus all costs associated with the repossession and sale. This debt can pursue you for many years after the house or other item has been sold.

Attachment of earnings

A creditor can apply to court to attach the wages of a debtor once a judgement has been entered. This can be a great shock for the unsuspecting debtor, as well as a source of great embarrassment. Unfortunately, it usually occurs at a time when everything else is going downhill financially. A typical example is of a young couple who were having severe financial difficulties. They had misused credit cards, store cards, hire purchase and so on. They were unable to meet all their obligations, and rather than face the creditors, they had taken the traditional ostrich approach. One of the creditors was a leasing company that specialised in contracts for furniture and appliances. Once their account was sixty days overdue, the leasing company moved swiftly and obtained a court order for repossession of the furniture. They then re-sold the furniture for a ridiculously low price and then sued the young couple for the deficiency, plus £400 in collection fees.

The couple were sent notices that the company was taking legal action but chose to ignore the warnings and did not go to court. Consequently, the company got an attachment of earnings order and attached both of their salaries. It was a shock when the young wife's boss called her into his office and showed her the order. The order required that the employer withhold up to five per cent of her wages to pay the judgement. For a family already having severe financial difficulties, that was a major crisis. The husband found that his wages were similarly attached.

Usually there is nothing that can be done once the judgement is finalised, but in this particular case it had a somewhat happier ending. After some checking around it was found that the leasing company had had several complaints filed against it for reselling repossessed furniture at prices substantially below the fair market value. Through a local solicitor the couple managed to get a new hearing at court and the judge withdrew the judgement and directed the leasing company to get three valuations on the furniture in question. The leasing company chose not to pursue the issue and dropped all collection proceedings against the couple. Thus the couple avoided the order but needed the next four years to work out their other financial problems. It later transpired that the judge had known the leasing company was suspect and would not have issued the judgement except that the couple didn't appear for the hearing and therefore he had no other choice. Sadly, this is true in so many cases – so if you are summoned to court go and put your side of the story.

Bad credit reference

Where a creditor cannot attach a debtor's wages and there are no funds in the bank for a garnishee order, no items for bailiffs to remove and no property on which to make a charging order, and the debt is unsecured (such as a credit card loan), the creditor has one last recourse: a bad credit reference and/or bankruptcy. Of course, creditors will pursue collection through notices and telephone calls, but in the final analysis they must rely on the integrity of the borrower.

The purpose of a credit reference is to notify other potential lenders that someone has failed to meet the conditions of a previous contract. The system relies on the fact that in our society people will need additional credit and thus will want to protect their credit rating. For a Christian the responsibility goes even further, because the requirement to repay a debt is one of personal honour and integrity. Nearly everyone in this country has information about them on file held by at least one of the major credit reference agencies. Whenever credit is applied for these are checked. Millions of people in this country are currently on a credit 'blacklist'. There are certain rights regarding this which include:

1. *The debtor has the right to know the name and address of the agency that prepared the report used to deny credit.* To obtain that information it is necessary to make the request to any creditor that has refused credit.
2. *Anyone refused credit has the right to review his file with the reference agency.* To obtain this information you need to send £1 to the agency concerned which has to send you a copy of your file within seven working days.
3. *Someone who is refused credit has the right to challenge the information in the report if he believes that it is inaccurate.* If the dispute cannot be resolved, a letter containing the debtor's version of the dispute (in under 200 words) can be placed in the file and can thus be seen by prospective lenders.
4. *Negative information cannot be reported beyond six years.*

Most creditors are willing to help anyone in financial trouble who is trying to be honest and repay what is owed. But when a debtor lies and defaults on commitments that were made, they are likely to find themselves faced with powerful and hostile adversaries. It is always best to be totally honest and not to make promises that cannot be kept just for the sake of temporary peace.

Few things make a better impression on a creditor than a well-thought-out budget plan, a list of all other creditors, and a credit card cut in half as a testimony of your commitment.

CHAPTER 17

LIVING WITH BANKRUPTCY

Is bankruptcy unscriptural?

That is not a simple question to answer. God's word clearly says that a believer should be responsible for his promises and repay what he owes. Does that mean that in the interim he should not take the legal remedy of court protection until he has the ability to repay? Often that is an individual decision. First, and foremost, a Christian must be willing to accept the absolute requirement to repay what he owes.

The issue of motive must be addressed. Is the action being taken to protect the legitimate rights of the creditors? We believe that answer can be found in asking whether or not assets are purposely withheld from the creditors. For example, many times when someone makes themselves bankrupt, assets have been transferred to the spouse or to other family members. If a husband and wife are treated as one, according to God's word, then their assets must also be treated as one.

Bankruptcy law is meant to protect the debtor and provide a fair distribution of money to creditors.

What about other court proceedings?

In the present generation it is not impossible or unlikely to be sued for millions of pounds over an accident. Also, given the present climate in jury decisions, it is not uncommon to be assessed huge damage awards. Is it scripturally acceptable then to make yourself bankrupt to deal with legal proceedings over an accident? Again, there are no easy answers to that question. A Christian who is faced with such a dilemma needs to pray about the situation when it happens and trust in God's guidance.

Of the many people who have undergone bankruptcy, some chose to do so voluntarily, and others had it forced upon them by their creditors. In both cases bankruptcy is a serious matter, and at best both sides lose. The creditors lose much of the money they are owed, and the debtors lose some of the respect they previously had. There is a stigma attached to bankruptcy, and until the last of the creditors are repaid it will probably remain. You can turn an otherwise negative situation into a positive one by making a commitment to repay what is legitimately owed. You can only do what you can do. Once you have made the commitment, it is then up to God to provide the means to do so.

Perhaps the scriptural principle that best describes the use of bankruptcy to avoid paying back legitimate debts is found in the parable of the unrighteous steward in Luke 16:1-12. In that parable the Lord describes a steward (a manager of another's property) who was guilty of misappropriating his master's property. When the master discovered what the steward had done, he determined to dismiss the steward. In an effort to maintain some security for himself, the manager negotiated with his master's clients and reduced the amounts they owed – apparently in the hope that they would pay him something later. When the master discovered that, he marvelled at the ingenuity of the deceitful manager (verse 8).

Does the Lord also marvel at one who goes bankrupt to avoid paying his creditors while holding assets that could be sold? Each Christian has to decide that issue individually, but what a shame it would be to appear before the Lord one day and learn, as Esau did, that he had traded his inheritance for a meal. Luke 16:13 says, 'No servant can serve two masters. Either he will hate the one and love the other, or he will be devoted to the one and despise the other. You cannot serve both God and money.'

CHAPTER 18

WHERE TO FIND HELP

The type of help a person in debt needs usually depends on the severity of the problems they are facing. If the problem is the overuse of credit cards and the total debt is a few hundred pounds, usually the solution can be worked out by working out a good plan. In that case what is needed is a commitment to avoid further debt and a budget to verify that commitment.

If a consolidation loan is needed to help bring the monthly payments in line with income, the help of a good counsellor is beneficial. The danger of going deeper into debt is increased by the additional loan unless some monitoring takes place. That's the primary role of the counsellor: to be an objective observer and provide accountability.

As the problems intensify, the need for professional help arises. If the monthly payments exceed the available income and a reduced payment plan is required, then a counsellor who will intercede is almost always a necessity. Often a well-trained counsellor can help negotiate reduced payments or a moratorium on some payments until assets can be sold. But if a negotiated settlement cannot be reached, then additional help is required. This may be a professional money adviser, an accountant or an insolvency practitioner.

Once the problems have reached the legal action stage, the need for outside counselling is essential. It is critical for a debtor to understand the rules of small claims courts or perhaps the bankruptcy court. That does not mean a debtor cannot handle any of those areas without professional help. With proper knowledge anyone can do so. However, Proverbs teaches us that a wise man seeks the counsel of others. 'Plans fail for lack of counsel, but with many advisers they succeed' (Prov 15:22). But another proverb tells us to weigh all advice carefully. 'A simple man believes anything, but a prudent man gives thought to his steps' (Prov 14:15).

Of great importance to the Christian is the admonition to avoid the direct advice of the non-Christian. That in no way implies that the non-Christian cannot give good financial advice. However, their advice is lacking the most essential element: God's word. It has been our experience that most advice from non-Christian financial advisers is aimed at protecting the assets of their clients, and that is to be expected. But a Christian must focus on the right of the other parties involved before his own. To do otherwise limits the ability of God to intercede on our behalf. Proverbs 3:5-6 says, 'Trust in the LORD with all your heart, and lean not on your own understanding; in all your ways acknowledge him, and he will make your paths straight.'

The primary source of any advice should be the local church. It is unfortunate, therefore, that most churches aren't equipped to provide financial counselling for their members, though more are getting trained to do so every year. Usually there are Christian accountants, bankers and business people within the church, who have the ability to help individuals with basic budgeting problems. If you need help, tell your pastor and ask him to refer you to someone in the church who can help on a volunteer basis. In general, most people are willing to help and are even flattered by such a request. Most importantly, your request may stimulate the church to begin providing this needed ministry on a regular basis.

Churches interested in starting a financial ministry can become part of a volunteer network established by Credit

Action, 6 Regent Terrace, Cambridge, CB2 1AA.

What can you expect from a counsellor? Too often those who ask for help expect too much too soon. Consequently, they become disillusioned when the counsellor doesn't have a magical formula that will make them debt-free in three months. Or, they expect the counsellor to tap the church treasury to bail them out of their troubles. In reality, fewer than twenty-five per cent of counselling cases (where the church was willing and able to assist financially) actually need direct financial support. With most of those, the financial help is temporary and only to meet basic needs. In most cases the answer for a couple in financial difficulties is personal discipline – not more money. There are obvious exceptions, such as families in which major illness has occurred, or elderly people who are living on fixed incomes that are lower than the poverty level. Those are needs that must be met by other believers and generally are not one-off needs.

If there are urgent needs, such as pending court repossession hearings, or evictions, we obviously need to try and deal with those immediately. But there are no guarantees. If a repossession or eviction is imminent, it may be that nothing can be done to forestall it. Usually an experienced counsellor will be able to advise about finding temporary housing but beyond that their function is counselling – not funding.

Many Christians expect unrealistic results from their advisers. Unfortunately, too many counsellors foster those expectations by presenting themselves as authorities on a great variety of topics ranging from sex to finances. Those assurances do help develop strong ties to the counsellor, but they are also self-defeating when the counsellees discover the hard truth that there is no substitute for personal discipline.

Those of us who have been doing financial counselling for several years sometimes think we have seen every possible problem and solution. Then someone comes up with an idea no one else has tried. Often when we pray with someone at the beginning of a counselling session, we are not really praying for them but for ourselves, realising that we do not know all the answers, but God does. If we can remember to draw from his wisdom, those we are counselling are not affected by our good or bad days.

One point must be made clear: God will not give us a direction in opposition to that which he has already given in his word. Thus the fundamental step is for an individual to understand what the word of God says. Once the rules for managing God's money are known, life becomes much easier for both the counsellor and the counsellee. If someone is not willing to follow the instructions given in God's manual, then the best counsellor in the world can't help him. A counsellor may deal with the immediate symptoms, but they will crop up again in a different place if the root problem is not resolved.

In Appendix 1 is a list of most of the scriptures dealing with the subject of credit. The minimum any Christian should do now is spend a few minutes a day looking at those scriptures and studying them. If he does that a couple of times, he will begin to get the message of what God's word has to say about credit. Credit is not prohibited, but it must be used properly.

Most counsellors at some time or another have been involved with a counsellee who has practically adopted them. The counsellee can become so dependent that they refuse to make any decisions without first consulting their counsellor. It becomes clear that these people have become so paralysed by their own mistakes, that they no longer trust their own judgement. Sometimes this is a predictable but temporary condition. For example, someone who has suffered a trauma such as a divorce or death of a spouse may well need the support of an adviser. But beyond a few weeks (at the very most), that can become a crippling dependency. We all need others from whom we can seek advice and confide in, but God must be our permanent source of support.

Some who are reading this book are probably depending

too much on a particular adviser. A counsellor is there to guide you and offer alternatives, but not to become a stand-in father or mother. Seek the face of God and his wisdom as your primary source of advice and you will never be disappointed. If you find that one of your counsellors is giving you advice which is contrary to God's word, seek another counsellor. Unless your counsellors understand the word of God, it is very likely that you will take the wrong action, even if you have the right motives. A good counsellor will take an objective look at the total financial picture and then make recommendations that will resolve the problems permanently. The basic counselling steps are as follows:

1. *Determine the actual spending level at present.* Rarely does a couple (or a single person) in debt know exactly how much it costs them to live each month. If they did, most would have already taken remedial action themselves. There are a variety of methods to determine how much they're presently spending. A good strategy is to begin by asking them to categorise how much they believe they spend each month (see Table 18.1 at the end of this chapter). Usually they have an estimated amount of spending, but rarely is it within fifteen per cent of the actual amount. Add a fixed percentage for many incidental expenses such as clothing, car repairs and holidays. Also if they have never lived by a budget, their miscellaneous spending may be as much as fifty per cent higher than they estimate.

2. *Ask the counsellees to keep a record of every expenditure for a month.* As you would expect, most couples in debt resist writing down every single purchase, but try to emphasise that this procedure is only necessary for one month – not for the rest of their lives. But it does require that each of them carry a pocket notebook for the month and write down every penny they spend. Once there is a clear picture of the actual monthly spending, the next step

is to develop a budget that will provide for all the regular household expenses with (hopefully) some money left over to pay creditors. As was discussed previously, this may require some adjustments in the living expenses – particularly in the areas of housing and cars.

3. *Ask the counsellees to maintain the budget each month.* There are no quick fixes for most people who experience financial problems. As our examination of the finances of several couples showed, each had different circumstances and required unique solutions. But one common denominator was the need to keep accurate records and control over their spending.

In solving financial problems, accountability is a key ingredient which cannot be overemphasised. The value of consistent accountability has been proved through Alcoholics Anonymous, Weight Watchers and Bible studies. The knowledge that someone will be checking to see if the bank account is balanced and the creditors paid helps to establish discipline.

Developing a support group in the community where you live can be a great asset to others who need help and accountability as well. Groups can meet as often as once a week to discuss their common problems and try to come up with practical solutions. They can also study what God's word has to say about the subject of finances and hold each other accountable to apply those principles.

Table 18.1
Monthly Income and Expenses

INCOME PER MONTH

		£
Salary		1,250.00
Benefits		
Other		
TOTAL GROSS INCOME		**1,250.00**
Less:	Tithe	125.00
	Tax	187.00

NET SPENDABLE INCOME   938.00

Housing	**391.00**	**Debts**		**90.00**
Mortgage (rent)	260.00	Credit Card		80.00
Electricity	28.00	Other Loan		10.00
Gas	52.00			
Water	11.00	**Entertainment &**		
Telephone	20.00	**Recreation**		**53.00**
Maintenance	20.00	Eating Out		20.00
		Babysitters		8.00
Food	**230.00**	Hobbies		10.00
		Trips		15.00
Car	**85.00**			
Petrol	40.00	**Clothes**		**50.00**
Insurance	20.00			
Tax	10.00	**Miscellaneous**		**99.00**
Maintenance/		Prescriptions		5.00
Replacement	15.00	Toiletries/cosmetics		10.00
		Hairdresser		20.00
Insurance	**39.00**	Laundry/dry cleaning		15.00
Life	29.00	Lunches		20.00
Medical	10.00	Gifts (including		
		Christmas)		25.00
		Subscriptions		4.00

TOTAL EXPENSES   1,037.00

INCOME vs EXPENSES
Net Spendable Income	938.00
Less Expenses	1,037.00
	−99.00

CHAPTER 19

DEBT-FREE LIVING – CHECK LIST

Emotions

Hitting the panic button

When debt strikes, your entire world can be turned upside down. And when that happens, it's the most normal thing in the world to hit the panic button. You might have been made redundant. You might have received a court summons because of an unpaid bill. You might have defaulted on your mortgage payment for the first time ever – or for the sixth month in a row. Your landlord might have started phoning you late at night to demand your overdue rent. Your gas might be disconnected, your TV or washing machine repossessed, or your children asked to leave their fee-paying school.

Any of these situations might be yours. In this no-man's land, most people are totally unprepared for what is happening and are completely unsure about what they should do next. Debt is a stigma. It frequently leads to shame, guilt and loneliness. Because of the pressure it brings, debt can force perfectly normal people to do very unusual things. One well-respected businessman committed suicide the day before his house was due to be repossessed. This came as a terrible shock to his wife – he had not told her a thing about their money problems.

Panic leads to at least three patterns of behaviour which go on to add to the problem:

- *Closing your heart* – redundancy and sudden debt makes you feel small. One man who suddenly lost his job after years with the same company said, 'You feel like you've been kicked in the stomach.' Shock usually leads to a sense of despair. You close your heart to hope and feel that you have been stripped of all dignity.
- *Closing your eyes* – others try to avoid despair by pretending that it's not really happening. In a terrifying situation such as debt, closing your eyes can seem like the best option – but it isn't. Some people carry on spending, or even binge. Others refuse to look all their debts in the face to see what their true situation is like.
- *Closing down* – many people caught in a crisis of debt cannot face those who are closest to them. Their partners, children, family and friends are left in the dark about what is going on. At the time when they most need the help and support of others, they simply close down.

If any of these descriptions match you, then please read on. These destructive patterns of behaviour can be changed for something better.

Opening your heart

If you are in despair because of your situation, you can take some comfort (however small) from the fact that you are facing reality. Many people try to pretend that everything is all right and try to put down their natural feelings of worry and fear.

You may have a number of different feelings about yourself, your creditors and your situation. You might feel frightened, insecure, angry, badly treated, powerless, lost, ashamed, lonely, hopeless or resigned. You have hit really hard times. All these feelings show that you are trying to come to terms with what has happened. You wouldn't be human if you didn't experience some or all of these feelings. But what can you do with feelings like these?

- *Try not to squash them* – take your feelings seriously, because they are registering that you have suffered a major blow. This is how God made you, as a living, feeling person.
- *Try to talk about how you feel* – if you keep your feelings to yourself, you could end up feeling very isolated and misunderstood. Knowing that others understand how you feel can be a great relief.
- *Try telling God how you feel* – God already understands your feelings, but turning to him in prayer lets you express yourself to God and draw comfort and strength from him. As the Bible says: 'Cast all your anxiety on him because he cares for you' (1 Pet 5:7). Don't be afraid to get angry with God or express your darkest feelings to him. There is no quick and easy healing for the pain you feel. You have to face some hard facts. You may never again know the standard of living which you once enjoyed. This is very tough – particularly in our society, which places such a strong emphasis on the status of wealth.

Real hope

The Bible gives no guarantees of an easy life but it does offer real hope. Whatever your circumstances, your true human worth and dignity lie with God. You may need a shift in your thinking to accept this. Perhaps you'll need to recognise that your security has always been built on a certain standard of living, rather than on God himself – the source of all security. Jesus once said: 'Do not store up for yourselves treasures on earth, where moth and rust destroy, and where thieves break in and steal. But store up for yourselves treasures in heaven … For where your treasure is, there your heart will be also'

(Mt 6:19-21). What does it mean to 'store up treasure in heaven?' Jesus is talking about a hope on which we can start to rebuild our lives.

Three promises from the Bible that can start to build hope

- *God made us and is with us* – he understands our lives from beginning to end. Read and pray through Psalm 139. Here are some of the things it says: 'Where can I go from your Spirit? Where can I flee from your presence? If I go up to the heavens, you are there; if I make my bed in the depths, you are there...'. God understands our thoughts and feelings and knows the true meaning of our lives.

- *God loves us and has a plan for us* – even in hard times, God still loves us. It can be hard to believe that God cares what is happening to us, when everything around seems to be collapsing. At one of their all-time low points, God's people in the Bible were promised: '"I know the plans I have for you," declares the LORD, "plans to prosper you and not to harm you, plans to give you hope and a future"' (Jer 29:11).

- *God hears our cries for help* – no matter how weak or powerless we feel in the face of debt, God hears us and sends us help. This doesn't mean that if we can only pray harder our debts will dissolve. God's help might come in many different ways: a new friendship, inner encouragement, a change in our circumstances, overcoming fear... 'I sought the LORD and he answered me; he delivered me from all my fears' (Ps 34:4).

However your debt crisis came about, you can come to see it as a test of your character and your faith in God. This is easy to put down in words, and much harder to live through – but it comes with a promise from the Bible: 'Blessed are those who persevere under trial, because when they have stood the test, they will receive the crown of life that God has promised to those who love him.'

Real hope takes time

If you are able to seize the new hope that God offers you, you will be in a much stronger position to start tackling your debt problems. New hope and new life do not come easily. You might need to repent and seek God's forgiveness. Or you might need to throw yourself on him because you have been hurt by the injustice of others. Whatever your need, as you read the Bible, take time to pray, and talk and pray with others, your life can be renewed from the inside.

Consequences of not facing up to debt

The worries about long-term debt show themselves in many different ways. They not only have a detrimental impact on the person concerned, but can have a devastating effect on those around you. It is so important to face up to the facts, to protect yourself and the ones you love, because constantly thinking about it can sap all your energy and bring you to breaking point. Here are some of the worst ways where untreated debt can strike:

● *Marriage breakdown.* Debt puts severe strain on relationships. Often one partner will feel guilty that he or she is in some way to blame. This will make him or her tense and moody. In many cases debt will go hand in hand with redundancy and, therefore, there is the added problem of lack of self-worth. In these depressed circumstances you may find yourself at home all day long, kicking your heels (and the cat) as you struggle to come to terms with what is happening. By being at home you could be disturbing your partner's routine, added to which it is unlikely that you will be very good company. In this situation it is hardly surprising that money worries are named as the number one cause of marriage break-up in over seventy per cent of cases.

● *Child abuse.* It is not only partners who suffer at times like this. Financial pressures can lead to stress at home and this can result in parents taking out their fears and frustrations on their children – especially if the children are making financial demands. The National Society for the Prevention of Cruelty to Children is only too well aware of this problem. Fortunately, not everyone in this situation resorts to violence, but some do and just one is too many. But many children are shouted at or neglected because of their parents' money worries.

- *Health problems.* It is becoming clear that debt is having a major impact in this area, with company welfare officers noting a marked increase in the number having to take time off work because of money worries. As they are probably fearful of losing their jobs as well, this really is a catch-22 situation. Debt can lead to stress, shock and depression and this is particularly true in the case of older people. Many who lose their jobs, or who see their standard of living drop sharply, lose their self-esteem. They see it as a blow to their dignity.

- *Loss of friends.* Because debt still carries a stigma, it is not discussed and as a result friendships are lost. Some friends will undoubtedly drift away, either because they feel debt is catching, or because a friend in debt is no longer of any use to them. These sort of 'friends' you can well do without. However, your real friends are people you can talk to and share your problems with. Just because you can no longer afford to entertain as you used to, or you are no longer able to buy your round of drinks, don't cut yourself off from them. True friends care for you and may well be able to offer all sorts of help – practical, emotional and sometimes even financial. Don't be too proud to accept. They are offering help because they genuinely want to, not because they are looking for something in return.

- *Despair and suicide.* It is important to recognise that a very small number of people have actually killed themselves because they allowed their debt problems to get out of control. In all the cases that I am aware of, the person concerned had not felt able to share their problems with anyone else. Yes, debt can make the future look hopeless – businesses fail and houses are repossessed. It can look as if you will be in debt for the rest of your life. But there is hope, and by reading this book you have taken the first step towards sorting things out. You have acknowledged that you have a problem.

Communication

With yourself

You might think that if being real about your situation will lead you into despair, then it's better to pretend. Better to carry on as if your debt crisis was simply not happening at all. Spend your way out of the crisis. Or perhaps you find that your life has simply switched on to autopilot. You no longer have the desire or strength to do something about your situation. Letters go unanswered, final demands heap up, phone calls are put off, and you find it hard to talk about it all. If this is how you are at the moment, then this section is here to flash a red warning light at you: you are in danger! If you fail to recognise what is happening and refuse to stop going through the red lights, you will very quickly hit disaster. At this point in your life, pretending and doing nothing are the very last things that can help you. There are several things you can do to open your eyes to where you are now.

● *Be real* – your first need is to face up to your situation, even though it is painful to do. One verse in the Bible says: 'Wake up! Strengthen what remains and is about to die...' (Rev 3:2). You might find that the best way to wake up is to confide in a friend, a church leader or counsellor. Tell them about how you feel, and why you find it difficult to face the facts. Simply talking about it will give you a better understanding of yourself, and the other person may be able to offer real help and support.

● *Act responsibly* – your mortgage, rent, tax and other money concerns are your responsibility (or a responsibility shared with your spouse). You need to take up your God-given responsibility to safeguard yourself and your family, and to honour your debts to the best of your ability.

With your family

Above all make sure that you are open and honest with your partner and any children who are old enough to understand. Let them know the full situation. After all, they are not going to adjust their spending patterns if they are unaware of a need to do so. It is important to share with them how you feel about what has happened and to let them express their feelings as well. If, for example, you have kept your family in the dark for a long time, it is very likely that you will be on the receiving end of considerable anger. Try to understand their feelings and give them time to allow the realisation of what has happened to sink in. Be prepared for this to take time. In some cases your partner may feel so let down by your inability to speak out sooner, that real pressures build up in your relationship. If this is the case, you will both need time for reconciliation and this may be impossible to achieve without independent, expert help, so don't be afraid of speaking to a third party. Remember that your partner is much more likely to be angry at your failure to speak out about the problem, than at the problem itself. Experience shows that men have much more difficulty in this area – so speak out as the situations develop.

With the benefits agency

It is important that everyone regularly checks that they are receiving all the benefits to which they are entitled, and this is particularly true of those whose circumstances have changed, eg. as a result of redundancy. Even government figures indicate that there are many people not claiming benefits to which they are entitled. It is a good idea to arrange an interview with a Benefits Adviser at your local Benefits Agency, and if you have been made redundant, it is vital that you sign on immediately. But you may well be entitled to other benefits as well. It is sensible to ask what benefits you can claim. They will then have to go into detail to see what, if anything, you can receive. Obviously you need to explain your circumstances fully if you are to receive all the benefits to which you may be entitled.

With creditors

If you are getting into financial difficulties you have a choice of what to do next. You can either ignore the problem, do absolutely nothing and just hope that your creditors don't notice that you have stopped paying your bills. It is so tempting to take this choice and simply hope that your money problems will disappear. But this will just not happen! You still start to get letters from your bank, building society or landlord. By not replying you will only make them more irate and far less likely to compromise in an effort to understand your situation. You could end up in court. You will certainly end up in a mess.

Alternatively, you have the option of letting your creditors know straight away that you are having difficulties making the repayments. By informing them as soon as possible you will avoid much distress, save time and usually receive sympathetic understanding. They can see that you are being honest, are wanting to tackle the problems and are trying to plan ahead as well as you can. The earlier you can do this the better, and it is well worth writing to them, even if you see a potentially dangerous cloud on the horizon which eventually blows away.

For example, you may fear that there are going to be some compulsory redundancies at your place of employment. You obviously hope that you are not going to be one of them, but it is good to take precautions just in case you are. In this sort of situation it is worth spending some time making a list of all the commitments you might struggle to meet if the worst comes to pass and then write to your creditors as soon as possible along the following lines:

Date   Your address

Creditor's name and address

Dear Sir or Madam

I am writing to inform you that it looks likely that there are going to be some compulsory redundancies at my place of work. I have to warn you that if I am made redundant I will experience considerable difficulty in paying my mortgage/rent/gas/electricity/Council Tax etc* It is unlikely, given the current economic climate, that I will obtain another job straight away, although I can assure you that I will be doing everything in my power to do so.

I am currently preparing my financial statement and will forward it to you as soon as it is ready. In the meantime if you have any suggestions that might help me meet my commitments to you more easily I would be delighted to hear them.

Obviously, if I do not lose my job I will continue to meet the payments to the best of my ability.

Thank you for your help.

Yours faithfully
(your name)

*Complete as appropriate

Remember, creditors are aware of what is happening in the economy. They know when recession or redundancy strikes. They will understand the financial pressures that sickness or divorce can bring. By keeping in touch and explaining your situation you stand a good chance of getting a helpful response.

The following quote from the Council of Mortgage

Lenders' guidelines entitled 'Handling of Mortgage Arrears' shows that this is so:

> 'When a borrower falls into arrears through no fault of his or her own, the problem is handled both sympathetically and positively. This requires that the borrower co-operates with the lender, in particular by reacting to correspondence.
>
> 'The key point in dealing successfully with arrears problems is that the borrower should make contact with the lender (or vice versa) at the earliest possible time. The borrower is likely to anticipate problems before the lender becomes aware of them. Lenders want borrowers to contact them before arrears begin to build up.'

With advisers

Very few of us have received more than a basic financial education. It makes a lot of sense therefore to seek advice as soon as danger looms. Be careful where you go. Friends may know no more than you do and some of their scare stories, which are probably totally unfounded, will not actually help. Some debt counselling agencies charge for their services. Others pretend to be debt counsellors but are really more like debt collectors. If in doubt – stay away. There are still places where you can get professional advice free of charge, although they are under immense pressure. Citizens' Advice Bureaux and Money Advice Centres are the most common. If you do decide to go, make sure you take all the necessary documents with you. Tell the adviser the position as clearly and quickly as possible. Be totally honest and do everything you are advised.

Remember that taking professional advice will almost certainly help your financial position. It should enable you to maximise your income, reduce interest levels and re-schedule payments. It should also prevent you receiving any undue harassment from creditors and should help prevent eviction and disconnection of utilities. Many of you will also avoid having to go to court if you take action soon enough and follow advice. There could be significant long-term advantages as well.

Knowing you are following good advice should improve both your physical and emotional well-being. There should be a feeling of relief that your problem is being shared, and a lessening of stress as well. This does not mean that your difficulties are going to disappear instantly. Recovery is often a long and arduous process, but at least you know there is help at hand when the unexpected comes along.

Budgeting

Budgeting is the art of keeping your spending under control. Like many things it sounds simple in theory, but can be really difficult in practice. How do you start to live within your means? Whether you currently have a debt problem or not, the quicker this can be done the better the situation will be, and you should start to feel greatly encouraged as you see your debts begin to decrease.

As budgeting has to be accurate, to be effective you need to keep track of everything. When you go shopping keep all the receipts and record where your money went as soon as you get home. Remember that odd visits to the pub, the sandwich shop and the office vending machine add up. You may well find that you are spending far more in these sorts of areas than you think you are. The simplest way to record all this expenditure is to keep a pocket-sized notebook with you so that you can record everything at the time you actually spend it. If in conjunction with this you accurately record on your cheque stubs what you have paid out, you should build up a very accurate account of your finances.

At this stage some of you may look at what is involved in budgeting and think it is just not worth while. You may think you have a very accurate picture of what you spend your money on. Without wanting to disillusion you, perhaps you would like to put this confidence to the test! Why not write down on a piece of paper what you think you or your family would spend on Christmas. Try and write down a figure straight away. Once you have done this look at 'Christmas Spending' and write in figures for each category. Then add up the total and compare it to the figure you had previously written down. If they are very similar you are either knowledgeable, lucky or dishonest!

It really is important that we compare these two figures. You see, as such there is no right or wrong answer to the question. But the outcome could be highly significant. If, for example, you thought you would spend £700 on Christmas, but when you added it up the total only came to £600, everything would be fine. You would actually have £100 left over. However, if you wrote down a figure of £500 and your actual spending added up to £1500, you would have got yourself into debt to the tune of £1000. And it is in these circumstances that you can almost guarantee that heavy gas and electricity bills would arrive at the same time.

Table 19.1
Christmas Spending

Presents	£
Cards	£
Postage	£
Decorations	£
Food	£
Drink	£
Fuel	£
Travel	£
Additional Telephone Calls	£
Other	£
CHRISTMAS SPENDING TOTAL	£

Hopefully this exercise will have convinced nearly everyone that there are several good reasons why you need to produce a budget:

● It will give you an accurate picture of your money situation.
● It could well enable you to reduce your spending and thus improve your overall position.
● It can be shown to creditors in an effort to convince them that your offer to them is fair and that you could not pay them any more.

When you budget it is important to remember a number of key things:

● *Be absolutely honest.* If you overstate your income or underestimate your expenditure (either by taking short cuts or missing things out because you think they aren't worth writing down) the only person you will fool is yourself. On this basis you may well make an offer to a creditor which is accepted that in reality you have no chance of paying. This will only infuriate the creditor, who may well give you no further chances of negotiation. So to prevent yourself getting into even deeper water, do make sure the budget is as accurate as you can make it.
● *Explore every option* that is available either to increase income or reduce expenditure. This can be very difficult and may only make a marginal degree of difference to your actual position, but if a creditor sees you are doing this, it is likely to influence his view of you considerably.
● *Involve all family members* who are old enough to understand. If other members of the family are consulted they are much more likely to help and work together to make the operation successful. It is important, too, to remember that although there are family priorities, there are individual priorities as well. Try not to criticise each other

too much, but end up with a budget that all your family are happy to try and stick to.

- *Keep your spending disciplined.* Your budget will soon be shot full of holes if you do not use it to guide your spending. Stick to the shopping lists you produce and try to cut out all impulse spending. Even 'small' items like magazines – perhaps a woman's monthly, a couple of sports or car glossies – can add up to £5 or more a time. If this £5 occurs each week, that's £20 a month or £260 a year.

- *Pay by instalments* whenever you can. Most things such as gas, electricity, TV licence, Council Tax, etc., that you are supposed to pay quarterly or annually, can now be paid on a monthly basis. It really is a good idea to do this wherever possible as it enables a more accurate picture to be built up month by month. It should also help reduce the number of unexpected or forgotten payments you will have to make.

- *Look at your statement carefully.* When you have finished, go over it once more. Can anybody think of anything that is missing?

Now that you have got the necessary principles, you need to start putting them into practice. The first thing to do is to add up all your *income*. Try to include everything here, including anything that your partner earns as well as any benefits you receive. It is best to ignore bonuses and overtime unless they are guaranteed, because if you include them and spend to the full, you could quickly find yourself in debt should they disappear.

Once you have calculated your income, you have to turn to your outgoings, and in essence you have to produce a list of everything your family spends money on in the course of a year. The first and largest area is your *formal commitments*. These include a variety of services you have to pay for on a monthly, quarterly or annual basis. Your mortgage/rent comes into this category, as do your electricity and gas bills, Council

Tax, car insurance and road tax. Remember to multiply all weekly payments by four and divide all quarterly ones by three. Annual payments are divided by twelve. By doing this you are ensuring all costs are looked at on a like-for-like basis, ie, monthly, especially if that is how you are paid.

After you have completed your formal commitments you need to look at your *everyday spending*. This is basically your food and grocery shopping, but also includes milk, newspapers, sweets, etc. By the way, one of the first things you need to do when budgeting is to acknowledge the difference between a 'need' and a 'want,' between an essential and a luxury. At the risk of alienating every reader it might look something like

Table 19.2

ESSENTIALS	LUXURIES
Mortgage/Rent	Telephone
Water Rates	TV Licence
Ground Rent	Car MOT
Council Tax	Road Tax
Property Insurance	Car Insurance
Contents Insurance	Personal Insurance
Electricity	School Fees
Gas	Toys and Books
Oil/Coal	Petrol
Maintenance	Parking
Basic Foodstuffs	TV Rental
Laundry/Dry Cleaning	Video Rental
Chemist	Cassettes/CDs
Public Transport	Hobbies
Essential Clothing	Newspapers
Dentist	Alcohol
Optician	Tobacco
Essential Repairs	Redecoration
	Trips Out
	Eating Out

This list should not be treated as 'correct.' Every individual will have different priorities, and for some people items such as telephone, car, television could appear in the first category. It is important, too, to remember to try and keep a little left over for some hobby or other form of escape.

Lastly you need to remember your *occasional costs*. These are largish items of expenditure that either come up at certain times of the year, like birthdays and Christmas, or else crop up unexpectedly, such as car repairs or decorating.

Using all the information you have received from your creditors, your notebooks and bank statements, work out your budget as accurately as possible. Remember not to include any payment you are currently making on existing debts. Apart from some of your occasional costs, which can be very irregular and impossible to quantify one hundred per cent accurately, you should have a budget that is very close to reality.

Table 19.3
Your Personal Budget

DETAILS OF MONTHLY INCOME

Your Basic Salary	Child Benefit
Spouse's Basic Salary	Income Support
Guaranteed Overtime	Family Credit
(Flexible Overtime)*	Other Benefits
(Flexible Bonuses)*	Maintenance
Pension	Disability Benefits
Other Income	**TOTAL £**

*Put in brackets but do not add to total as these figures cannot be relied on week after week. When they occur, use to pay off debts or save as appropriate.

DETAILS OF MONTHLY EXPENDITURE

Formal Commitments

Tithe	£	Car MOT	£
Mortgage	£	Road Tax	£
Rent	£	Vehicle Insurance	£
Water Rates	£	Regular Savings	£
Ground Rent	£	Personal Insurance	£
Council Tax	£	Private Pension	£
Property Insurance	£	Maintenance Payments	£
Contents Insurance	£	Second Mortgage	£
Electricity	£	Loan Repayments	£
Gas	£	HP Repayments	£
Oil	£	Credit Card	
Coal	£	Repayments	£
Telephone	£	School Fees	£
TV Licence	£	Other	£

FORMAL COMMITMENTS – TOTAL 1   £

Everyday Spending

Food	£	Public Transport	£
Sundries	£	TV Rental	£
Baby Maintenance	£	Video Rental	£
Children's Pocket Money	£	Evening Classes	£
Childminder	£	Sports/Hobbies	£
Toys and Books	£	CDs and Tapes	£
Pet Food	£	Alcoholic Drinks	£
Laundry/Dry Cleaning	£	Cigarettes/Tobacco	£
Chemist	£	Newspapers/Magazines	£
Petrol	£	Other	£
Parking	£		

EVERYDAY SPENDING – TOTAL 2   £

Occasional Costs

Christmas	£	Vet Bills	£
Birthdays	£	Clothing	£
Holiday	£	Dentist	£
Subscriptions	£	Optician	£
Car Repairs	£	Trips and Outings	£
House Repairs	£	Meals Out	£
Redecoration	£	Other	£
Replacement Furniture	£		

OCCASIONAL COSTS – TOTAL 3   £

TOTAL 1	£
TOTAL 2	£
TOTAL 3	£

GRAND TOTAL	£

BALANCE
Monthly Income   £
Monthly Expenditure   £

Monthly Surplus   £

How does it look? At this stage you will really be hoping that there will be some surplus, however small, to help you start repaying your debts. But even if that is not the case, all is not lost. For example, you are now in a position where, with your budget completed, you can send a letter to your creditors which fully explains your situation. If you have no surplus, you can ask for breathing space while you try and improve your situation.

It is important to remember at this stage that even if you don't like what you see, and you think your creditors won't either, then it is still important to keep them informed. They may be rude or unhelpful, but they will be far more so if you fail to make and keep contact.

In conclusion

If you follow the above procedure, budget sensibly and spend wisely you should be on your way to a life of debt-free living.

CREDIT RELATED SCRIPTURES*

Subject:	Scripture:	Comments:
Borrowing	Exodus 22:14	Restitution for borrowed property
	Exodus 22:15	No restitution for rented property
	Deuteronomy 28:43-45	Disobey God and become borrower
	Nehemiah 5:2-5	Jews borrowing from Jews
	Psalm 37:21	Wicked does not repay
	Proverbs 22:7	Borrower is lender's slave
	Isaiah 24:2	Borrower will be like lender
Lending	Exodus 22:25	Lend to brothers without interest
	Deuteronomy 15:6	Lend but do not borrow
	Deuteronomy 28:12	Obey God and lend

*Condensed from *A Topical Concordance on Finances* by Larry Burkett (Christian Financial Concepts, 1989)

	Psalm 37:26	Godly man lends
	Psalm 112:5	God blesses lender
	Isaiah 24:2	Borrower will be like lender
	Jeremiah 15:10	I have not lent
	Ezekiel 18:7	Restore pledge to borrower
	Ezekiel 18:8	Does not lend at interest
	Ezekiel 18:12	Evil retains pledge
	Ezekiel 18:13	Lends at interest
	Ezekiel 18:16-17	Does not keep pledge
	Habakkuk 2:6-7	Woe to those who lend at interest
	Luke 6:34-35	Lend, expecting nothing
Interest	Deuteronomy 23:19	Do not charge interest to a brother
	Deuteronomy 23:20	May charge foreigner interest
	Psalm 15:5	Do not charge interest
	Proverbs 22:26-27	Don't sign pledges
	Proverbs 28:8	Wrong to lend at interest
	Ezekiel 18:7	Godly returns pledge
	Ezekiel 18;8	Godly does not charge interest
	Ezekiel 18:12	Wicked keeps pledge
	Ezekiel 18:13	Wicked charges interest
	Ezekiel 18:16-17	Godly does not charge interest
	Ezekiel 18:18	Ungodly extort from poor
Usury	Leviticus 25:35-37	Do not charge a brother usury
	Nehemiah 5:7-10	Charging a brother usury
	Proverbs 28:8	Usury will revert to God

Surety	Genesis 43:9	Surety for Benjamin
	Genesis 44:32	Surety for Benjamin
	Exodus 22:26	Return a pledge
	Deuteronomy 24:10-13	Do not keep poor man's pledge
	Job 22:6	Has taken a pledge from brothers
	Psalm 109:11	Seize all a debtor has
	Proverbs 6:1-3	Beg to be released from surety
	Proverbs 11:15	Surety for a stranger
	Proverbs 17:18	Ignorant becomes surety
	Proverbs 20:16	Ignorant pledges cloak as surety
	Proverbs 21:27	Sacrifice of wicked
	Proverbs 22:26-27	Do not become surety
	Proverbs 27:13	Take his garment
Paying Debts	Genesis 38:20	Judah paid harlot
	Deuteronomy 15:1-5	Seven-year remission of debts
	Deuteronomy 31:10	Year of remission of debts
	2 Kings 4:1	Widow's children for debts
	2 Kings 4:7	Elisha pays widow's debt
	Proverbs 3:27-28	Pay when debt is due
	Matthew 5:25-26	Make friends of lenders
	Luke 12:58-59	Make friends of lenders
	Romans 13:8	Do not be left owing
	Colossians 2:14	Cancel debts
	Philemon 18,19	Paul offers to pay debts

BENEFITS

There are two ways to correct a domestic budget deficit – cut expenditure or boost income. It is always wise to consider whether income can be boosted because of an entitlement to additional state benefits.

An example:

Mr M was in very low paid work. He worked full-time and unsociable hours for about £85 per week. His wife had had a brain tumour many years previously. The couple had six children. The only other income the family had was family credit (£115 per week) and child benefit (£53 per week), giving a *total income of £253*. Mr M had about £3000 of arrears on his first mortgage. The building society had begun possession proceedings and he had been backwards and forwards to court, avoiding actual repossession by the skin of his teeth. He had a second mortgage. This lender had also started possession proceedings. Then Mr M lost his job.

Following the intervention of an advice centre, Mrs M now receives both Severe Disablement Allowance and Disability Living Allowance. The couple receive income support at a higher rate than normal because of Mrs M's illness. The couple's *total income is now £342*. A year after Mr M lost his job, mortgage arrears had fallen to about £700. Other unsecured debts had been repaid and Mr M was keeping to an arrangement to repay Council Tax arrears off at £10 per week.

*

Now few individuals or couples will be missing out on as much as £90 per week and few will have their financial position changed so dramatically by claiming additional benefits. Indeed, for many, there will no benefit entitlement whatsoever. However, for a significant number a benefits check will reveal possibilities for boosting income.

To claim or not to claim

Many people, especially older people, are proud of never having claimed state help. That is understandable. It is a good thing to be able to support one's family by one's own labours. Because of this attitude, when a crisis arrives some people feel a deep embarrassment about claiming benefit. In some cases the embarrassment is so great that available help is not claimed. However, this kind of extreme embarrassment is not appropriate.

In many cases, all benefit does is bring the claimant's income up to the breadline. If the benefit is not claimed, the person and his family are left in absolute poverty so that there will be insufficient income to meet basic needs, let alone cover payments to creditors. If benefit is not claimed, the individual's debt problem is likely to deepen, causing far greater embarrassment.

And embarrassment about claiming benefits is not necessarily reasonable. Entitlement to many benefits is based upon previous payment of national insurance contributions. The contributions paid are just like an insurance premium. When a proper insurance claim is made to the Benefits Agency (the part of the DSS that deals with benefit claims), the claim is met.

No one who has their house burgled has the slightest embarrassment about putting in a claim to their insurance company. Why should there be any embarrassment about claiming against the national insurance scheme?

Admittedly, entitlement to some benefits is not linked directly to payments of national insurance contributions. Nevertheless, the claimant or his/her family have often paid taxes for many years. Those taxes were used, in part, to help other citizens in need. There is nothing wrong with receiving assistance in turn, when help is needed.

Finally, there is often a particular embarrassment for those who need to claim benefit because of unemployment. Unfortunately, attacks by a few politicians on the limited number who abuse the system, have made many legitimate claimants feel like scroungers. No doubt society can reasonably expect people to do what they can to find work. Nevertheless in a world with a shortage of employment opportunities, the unemployed should not be blamed for their misfortune.

Society as a whole has a problem. We have not managed to organise ourselves in such a way as to provide full employment. Those in work benefit at the expense of those out of work: the jobs that those of us in work have are available because the unemployed are not in them! Surely then, the legitimately unemployed deserve to be compensated for the fact that they carry the burden of society's problem and should not be embarrassed by their misfortune.

Golden rules

There is a limit to the amount of specific information about benefits which can be included in a short appendix. There are, however, some straightforward 'golden rules' to remember:

1. You don't get if you don't ask

Generally speaking there is no harm in applying for a benefit.

In the vast majority of cases, the worst that can happen is that the claimant is refused the benefit. But see below about seeking specialist advice first.

If you ask for a claim form, you should always be given one or sent one. A telephone request for a form will usually suffice. Keep a written note of the date and time you made the request. Ask the Benefits Agency officer you speak to for his or her name. Some of the forms are quite long and intimidating. If the claimant does not understand all the questions or can't answer all of them, s/he should fill in as much as s/he can, sign and date the form and send it back. The Benefits Agency will write to the claimant to try to get more information, but they will, most probably, accept the claim as running from the date the form was submitted.

2. Don't believe everything you're told

Different benefits are administered by different Benefits Agency offices. In the case of housing benefit and council tax benefit, the claims are dealt with by local authorities. The new Jobseekers' Allowance, which replaced Unemployment Benefit and income support for the unemployed from 7 October 1996, is administered by the Employment Service at Job Centres. If a member of the public rings a particular Benefits Agency office, s/he may speak to an officer who does not normally deal with the benefit in question. If the officer is sensible, s/he will refer the caller on. However, it is the experience of advisers working in the field that erroneous opinions are often given in these circumstances.

Example:

Mrs Z was taken seriously ill by a rare virus. She was paralysed for some weeks and left with acute breathlessness. She could not walk more than a few yards. Mr Z approached the Employment Service to ask what benefits might be available to him and his wife as he had to give up work to look after her. He was told nothing was available because the couple had savings. This advice was wrong. Mrs Z could have claimed Disability Living Allowance on account of her poor mobility and would quite possibly have been entitled to the benefit for the rest of her life. As it was, by the time Mr and Mrs Z got correct advice, Mrs Z had turned sixty six years old and was too old to claim this benefit. As a result of poor advice, she had lost the opportunity of receiving over £30 per week for the rest of her life.

*

Even where an inquirer speaks to an officer who does deal with a particular benefit, mistakes are commonly made. For a start, social security law is highly complicated. In an important case in the Court of Appeal, Lord Justice Glidewell said that:

> Even for this legislation, [the provisions in question] are particularly obscure in their meaning ... it is deplorable that legislation which affects some of the most disadvantaged people in society should be couched in language which is so difficult for even a lawyer trained and practising in this field to understand.[1]

Secondly, Benefits Agency staff are of varying degrees of knowledge and competency. Internal training varies in standard. Benefits Agency offices are generally under-resourced and staff are hard-pressed. This is an environment where mistaken advice can easily be given.

Finally, there is the matter of the bureaucratic culture of Benefits Agency offices and Council offices. Sometimes, offices or sections within offices display a culture of scepticism and suspicion towards claimants. Assumptions are

---

[1] Bate v Chief Adjudication Officer and Secretary of State for Social Security, *The Times* 12.12.94, quoted in the Preface of CPAG's *Income Related Benefits: The Legislation* by Mesher and Wood.

made either about claimants or about the law without proper investigation.

Example:

On one occasion a local Benefits Agency office would not accept that neither parent of a disabled child was required to sign on as available for work in order to get income support. The father was pressurised to sign on. Only later did the Benefits Agency concede that he did not have to. In explanation, the Benefits Agency officer said that he simply could not believe that the law did not require the father to sign on.

*

3. Seek Advice

Social security matters are very complicated. If at all possible, it is wise to seek advice. A specialist adviser can give advice about benefit entitlement. An adviser can help an individual to make the informed choices about which benefits to claim, what information needs to be supplied to the Benefits Agency, and the best way to frame that information. A specialist can also advise about whether Benefits Agency decisions are correct or lawful and about the options for taking a case further.

Specialist help can be obtained from the following sources:

- *Council Welfare Rights' Officers.* Some Councils employ staff to advise the public, or perhaps sections of the public with special needs, about benefits. You can find out whether a Council has Welfare Rights' Officers by ringing the Council's Social Services Department.
- *Citizens' Advice Bureaux.* Some CABx have well-qualified, paid, advisers who will normally be able to give good quality advice. However, some CABx expect their ordinary volunteers to give welfare benefits advice. It would be fair

to say that the quality of this advice varies.

- *Other Advice Centres and Law Centres.* Many of these have experienced welfare rights' workers.
- *Private Solicitors.* A very few solicitors specialise in this area. Those that do will generally give high quality advice. Other solicitors will quite likely know little or nothing about the benefits system. So it is unwise to seek advice from a High Street solicitor, unless the solicitor is a known specialist. CABx should be able to advise which firms of solicitors specialise in benefits law.

Of course, private solicitors normally have to be paid. However, if an individual or his/her partner is already receiving income support, means-tested jobseekers' allowance or family credit, or has a very low income, the Legal Aid Board will usually pay the solicitor's fees, so that the client does not have to pay. Even if a person falls outside of the scope of legal aid, some solicitors will give initial free interviews or £5 fixed fee interviews. Whatever happens, if a person goes to see a solicitor, the first thing the solicitor should do is advise about his fees and give the client an opportunity to leave there and then if the client cannot afford to meet the fees. So in that sense, there should be no risk involved in going to see a specialist solicitor to ask if they can help.

4. Don't Necessarily Accept 'No' For An Answer

Very many people who receive a benefit were initially turned down by the Benefits Agency. Many decisions call for the adjudicator to make fine judgements which are often overturned by way of internal Benefits Agency reviews or on appeal. If a claimant feels uneasy about a decision, s/he should seek specialist advice promptly. In the absence of specialist help, a disappointed claimant should consider appealing anyway.

Many Benefits Agency decisions can be appealed. Appeals are heard by independent tribunals. Tribunal hearings are quite informal and designed to be user friendly. The tribunal will usually take a completely fresh look at the question and substitute its own decision for that of the Benefits Agency adjudicator. Claimants have the right to attend appeals and give oral evidence and a right to be represented by a lawyer or adviser. Claimants who attend appeal hearings are more likely to succeed than claimants who do not. And claimants who are represented are more likely to succeed than those who attend unrepresented.

The benefits

Benefits for rich and poor alike

Some benefits are paid regardless of income and savings and regardless of whether any national insurance contributions are paid. The most common of these is child benefit (the old family allowance). Entitlement is based more or less solely upon having a child under sixteen or under nineteen and in school or FE college.

- *One-parent benefit* is also non-means-tested. Because it is non-means-tested, a single parent who starts working can keep this benefit (or claim it).
- *Attendance Allowance* is for older people with care needs or who need supervision. Disability Living Allowance is for younger people with care/supervision needs or for those under sixty-six with mobility problems. Children can be entitled to this benefit. It can be claimed, for instance, for a child with acute asthma, eczema or even bed-wetting, if the child has significant care needs. Invalid Care Allowance is paid to those who spend a significant part of the week caring for someone else. Again, this caring can be for a sick child as well as for an adult.
- *Severe Disablement* Allowance is paid to some people who are unfit for work but not entitled to incapacity benefit (see over).

Benefits for National Insurance Payers

Most employed or self-employed people are obliged by law to pay national insurance contributions. These contributions confer benefits. These benefits were originally designed to replace income in the event of retirement, sickness and unemployment. These days, these benefits do not stretch very far.

Perhaps most importantly, national insurance contributions can add up towards a state retirement pension. A full contribution record affords a full pension. Contributions made in recent years can also count towards incapacity benefit and non-means-tested jobseekers' allowance (which replaced unemployment benefit). If the contribution conditions are satisfied, these benefits are paid regardless of the income and savings of the claimant.

Means-tested Benefits

These benefits are designed to deal with poverty. The amount of benefit is arrived at by comparing the income that the individual or family has with the government's assessment of the family's need. The need figure is a standard figure reflecting the size of the family, age of its members and, in some cases, the housing costs of the family.

To be entitled to means-tested jobseekers' allowance, an individual and his partner must not work for more than a certain number of hours per week. The claimant must be available for work and actively seeking work and will have to enter into a jobseekers' agreement. The amount of benefit is the sum needed to raise income up to the need figure (called the applicable amount).

Income support is available in situations where an individual or one of a couple is exempt from the normal requirement to look for work. Usually this is because of sickness or retirement or because the claimant is a carer. Again the amount of benefit is calculated by subtracting the family's income from the size of their need.

Housing benefit is intended to help meet rent, and council tax benefit is, not surprisingly, to help meet the cost of the council tax. If a person receives means-tested jobseekers' allowance or income support, they are normally entitled to 'full' housing benefit up to a maximum figure for the property in question, and council tax benefit sufficient to meet one hundred per cent of their council tax liability. (The position is different if there other adults living in the same household eg, adult children.)

This 'full' housing benefit may not be equivalent to the actual rent. A shortfall between maximum housing benefit and actual rent can cause acute hardship, because income support and jobseekers' allowance are designed only to meet the barest of necessities and they are not intended to cover rent costs.

If a person is not entitled to jobseekers' allowance or income support, a comparison is made between need (the applicable amount) and income. The crucial figure is the amount by which income exceeds need. An individual or family is expected to contribute sixty-five per cent of this excess towards their housing costs and twenty per cent of this excess towards council tax and benefit is paid to make up the difference.

Family Credit is available to families where one partner (or a single parent) is working for a certain number of hours per week. It is intended to boost the income of low-paid workers.

It should be borne in mind that Family Credit does not provide assistance towards mortgage interest costs. Jobseekers' allowance and income support often do. This means that a claimant and his/her family can be significantly worse off when a claimant finds work and switches from jobseekers' allowance to Family Credit. In spite of this, it is unlikely that a Job Centre officer will accept this reduction in income as justification for refusing to accept a job.

People who don't claim who could

There may be a large amount of benefits fraud, but there is an even larger amount of unclaimed benefit. Latest official estimates show:

- Unclaimed income support between £740 million and £1.66 billion.
- At least 700,000 people entitled to income support were not claiming.
- At least one in four pensioners who were entitled to income support were not claiming.
- Nearly thirty per cent of those entitled to Family Credit were not claiming.
- At least 1.34 million not claiming council tax benefit to which they were entitled.

Underlying these figures, certain groups commonly miss out on benefits they are perfectly entitled to.

- *Pensioners.* A standard state pension is no longer large enough to bring a pensioner's income up to the breadline. If a pensioner has no other source of income and has only modest savings, he/she will normally be entitled to some income support. This income support may only be a few pounds per week, but it could amount to a significant sum if the pensioner still has a mortgage on his/her home.
- *Self-employed.* The self-employed are entitled to Family Credit in the same way that those in low-paid work are. Family Credit can be crucial in the early stages of a new business venture.
- *Couples where the wife/female partner is ill.* If the husband/male partner is working, the woman may be entitled to Severe Disablement Allowance regardless of her partner's income.

Things to think about

Mortgages.

Buying a house is not risk free. If a home owner's income falls dramatically, how will the mortgage be paid? There is only limited help from the Benefits Agency. The Benefits Agency sometimes makes payments to cover mortgage interest. It never makes payments to cover capital repayments or endowment policy premiums. If a mortgage was taken out before 2 October 1995, eight weeks into a claim the Benefits Agency will cover fifty per cent of interest on certain types of loans (broadly speaking loans used to buy the property or for certain types of repairs or improvements). Twenty-six weeks into a claim, the DSS pays all the mortgage interest on certain types of loans. For loans taken out after 1 October 1995, no payments are made towards interest for the first thirty-nine weeks whatever the type of loan. After thirty-nine weeks, one hundred per cent of interest can be met on certain types of loans.

In the light of the above:

1. *Hesitate when re-mortgaging a property.* If an old loan is being paid off by a new loan, the right to half mortgage interest from eight to twenty-six weeks, and full interest thereafter, will probably be lost, and instead, in the event of an income support claim, no payments towards interest will be made until the fortieth week of a claim.

2. *If a secured loan was used for non-home related matters,* eg. car, caravan, holiday, or to pay off other high interest debts, the DSS will not contribute towards interest repayments. On income support, it will be nigh on impossible to service the loan. And if the loan is not serviced, the loan company will probably try to repossess the home. Secured loans are not good loans to default on!

3. *Think carefully before taking on an endowment mortgage.* These mortgages are less flexible if things go wrong and a family is on income support. If the premiums are not paid, the endowment policy may be terminated. A small amount may be paid back to the borrower, but probably less than the total premiums paid. In other words, a lot of money can be lost. However, if someone has a repayment mortgage

and their income drops, it may be possible to negotiate a freeze of capital repayments until income rises again. In this way no money is lost.

Remember that a couple cannot claim benefit

One spouse/partner must claim for both. Normally, the husband/male cohabitee will be the claimant. However, it may make more sense for the wife/female partner to claim. For a couple to get money, the claimant either has to sign on as available for work, or has to be exempt (eg. because they are unfit for work or a full-time carer). If the wife /female partner is exempt from the need to sign on, she can claim and there is no need for the husband/male partner to claim.

Additionally, the couple could be significantly better off if the exempt partner claims. In circumstances where a husband is signing on and claiming benefit, but where the wife has been ill for at least a year, the couple would probably be £30 per week better off if the claimant role was swapped and the husband would not need to sign on every fortnight in order to get benefit.

The Benefits Agency and local authorities can take a long time to process claims

This can be a real problem for those in debt. It is bad enough facing a drop in income; but it is a lot worse to have no income at all! The Benefits Agency is usually reasonably good at dealing with straightforward claims. However, if the claim is a little complicated or the claimant presents an unusual set of circumstances, delays are not uncommon. Where there are delays, we suggest the following:

1. *If there has been no response within fourteen days, contact the Benefits Agency office.* Sometimes the office will deny receipt of the claim. If this is the case, deliver a copy straightaway. (This is just one reason why it is very important to keep a copy of an application if at all possible.)

2. *If the claim has been received, but not dealt with, ask for an explanation.* If the explanation is unsatisfactory, make a complaint. This can be done by writing to the Customer Services Manager at your Benefits Agency office.

3. *Ask for an interim payment while the claim is being sorted out.* If this is refused, contact your MP and ask for his/her help.

If the claim is for housing benefit or council tax benefit, then it will be administered by the local authority. Unfortunately, many local authorities have a very poor record for administering claims quickly and efficiently. Many new tenants run up considerable rent arrears before claims for housing benefit are processed. This is a particular problem because some landlords will seek to evict the tenant for arrears.

As with income support, it is theoretically possible to obtain interim payments. Indeed, unlike the Benefits Agency, Councils are obliged by law, in certain circumstances, to make interim payments. If the Council has failed to process a claim by a private tenant after fourteen days, and that is not down to the claimant's failure to supply information, then an interim payment should be made. Unfortunately, many local authorities act as if the interim payment rules do not exist. Many authorities never make an interim payment unless they are threatened with Court action. Such is the disregard for the law that some housing benefit officers working for Councils seem honestly ignorant that the law requires interim payments to be made.

We advise that all requests for further information received by the Council are answered promptly. As soon as the claim has been in the Council's hands for fourteen days, a request should be made for an interim payment. If an immediate response is not forthcoming, a complaint should be made. You should also consider seeking legal advice from a solicitor specialising in welfare benefits law, or a Law Centre if there is one in your area. A solicitor may be able to apply for legal aid to sue the Council to force it to make an interim payment. You could also try to involve your local councillor and you could make a complaint to the Local Ombudsman.

BANKRUPTCY

What are my options when I'm in debt?

If you have outstanding debts that you can't pay as they should be paid, there are various options:

- Do nothing
- Make an offer to your creditors: either a non-statutory arrangement; or an Individual Voluntary Arrangement under the Insolvency Act; or apply to the court for a County Court Administration Order.
- Bankruptcy: either a creditor or you applying.

These options are looked at below.

Even if you feel that the following notes are sufficient for you to know what you want to do, you are likely to benefit from the advice of a debt counsellor or adviser, or an insolvency practitioner. One or more of the options may be of financial benefit to the adviser. You should know if that is the case, and also ensure that you obtain all the information you need about all the options available to you. You will find telephone numbers and addresses of the various advisers in most local telephone and other directories.

Do nothing

There may be physical, emotional and other personal reasons why you are unable to deal with your situation. In that case you may wish to consider whether you should seek assistance and/or whether there is someone you can trust sufficiently to act on your behalf to deal with your financial problems. You need to be aware of the likely results of doing nothing about your debts:

1. Your creditors will not know of your situation and may, therefore, presume the worst of you.
2. Each of your creditors may continue to do their utmost to get money from you, using whatever legal means are available, such as:

● Obtaining a court judgement against you.
● Obtaining information about you, your income and what you own. They can do this by: looking at any papers which you may have signed for them; instructing enquiry agents; asking the court to make an order for an 'Oral Examination' at which you would be asked questions to discover what you are able to pay.
● Each of your creditors may use the following methods to enforce their claim: bailiffs removing your non-essential goods; obtaining an order for your employer to make payments directly out of your wages or salary; a Charging Order on a property owned by you; an order taking money from your bank account (garnishee); apply for your bankruptcy.

What offer can I make?

Your creditors want as much of their money as quickly as possible, and they also want to know in advance what they can expect to receive. Your best offer to your creditors will include all the following, if available:

- Regular payments out of surplus income.
- Any 'windfalls'.
- Any lump sum of money you have now, and money from the sale or surrender (or remortgage) of any valuable items.
- Payments to continue until you have paid in full, unless that is an unreasonably long period. (Some say that seven years is the limit.)
- Details of how you have come to be in your current situation.

If you make the best possible offer to a creditor, who then refuses it, a court will be much more likely to refuse to make an order against you in bankruptcy or enforcement proceedings if asked to do so by that creditor.

One of the most important pieces of information your creditors will want is a list of your income and expenditure, so that they know how much surplus income you have to offer. It is crucial that you think very carefully before you fill in an income and expenditure sheet to ensure that you have included all your expenditure. It may be impossible, later on, to insert an additional category. Creditors will wish to limit your household expenditure to 'necessary' expenditure. Experience shows that each creditor will have different standards as to what they consider 'necessary'. Creditors will expect a review of the amount you can afford to pay at least once, and possibly twice each year.

Non Statutory Arrangement (debt management plan)

This is an offer to your creditors to pay them what you can afford. There are no courts or court costs involved, and there is no advertisement or registration process as there is with an IVA (see below). Every one of your creditors will have to agree to your offer, although some advisers do not make a formal offer, but instead simply tell the creditors what is happening, ie they are to receive reduced 'pro rata' payments.

It may take a number of weeks, or even months, because of the procedures of creditors' recovery departments, before all the creditors finally respond to accept or reject your offer. During the period after an offer is sent to the creditors, you may find that you continue to receive letters and notices from creditors and debt collectors pressing you for payment. A court may still make a 'judgement' against you during this period, which is likely to be registered at the County Court Judgement Registry.

It is likely to be very difficult, if not impossible, to deal with business debts or income tax, or other statutory debts, using a non-statutory arrangement with creditors.

County Court administration order

Under this procedure the court will collect the regular payments which you can afford to make out of your income, take a fee of ten per cent, and distribute the remainder to your creditors. An order can be made if you have debts of less than £5,000 and a County Court Judgement against you. For further information you should speak to your local county court office.

Individual Voluntary Arrangement (IVA)

An IVA is a convenient way of getting all your creditors to agree an arrangement, especially since it is often difficult to persuade every single creditor to agree to an informal arrangement. The section below entitled *Disadvantages of Bankruptcy* sets out various reasons why people need to avoid bankruptcy. If you are in that position, an IVA may be the only way to proceed.

In an IVA, an offer to the creditors will generally be accepted provided:

● Nothing which it is reasonable to include is left out.
● Nothing is hidden.
● It is seen to be reasonable.

● Your history with the creditors makes you credible to them.

The offer will include as many of the features as possible mentioned under the section *What Offer Can I Make?*, such as regular payments out of your income, the sale of something of value, a lump sum made available by a member of the family, etc.

The IVA should be in full and final settlement of all your debts, and has to be set up and supervised by an insolvency practitioner. The courts have a general overseeing role, and an application is necessary for an 'Interim Order'. Any creditor who is left off your list of creditors will not be bound by your IVA, and may not be able to 'join in' at a later stage, so everyone must be included. This may be a good reason not to propose an IVA if there is a creditor (such as your employer) who you don't want to learn about your financial difficulties.

The creditors are invited to a meeting to vote to accept or reject your proposal to them, and all of them will be bound by the result of the meeting. Your proposal will be approved if seventy-five per cent in value of the creditors who attend the meeting vote to accept it. The chairman of the meeting is allowed to adjourn a meeting for up to, but no more than, fourteen days, to obtain an approval. The creditors' response will, therefore, be known relatively quickly. If the IVA is approved, it has to be registered, and it is normal practice for credit reference agencies to include that information on their files for six years.

Whatever you offer to the creditors in an IVA should normally include costs with nothing else to pay. However, because of the extra initial cost of setting up an IVA (compared with a non-statutory arrangement – see above) an insolvency practitioner will usually ask for a payment in advance before starting work, and this advance payment will be lost if the creditors reject your proposal to them.

An IVA cannot replace the need to continue to pay:

- Mortgage instalments and ongoing rent.
- HP and lease instalments, electricity, gas, water, telephone.
- Suppliers or services needed to enable you to continue to receive your income.
- A fine, for which you would risk imprisonment if you did not pay.
- Any further debts after the start of the arrangement.

Bankruptcy

The purpose of bankruptcy is to get money for your creditors: from everything of value of yours; from any 'surplus' income you may have until you are discharged; from any unexpected money or property which you receive until you are discharged.

The creditors no longer come after you for your debts – they only have a claim for the money which comes into your bankruptcy if there is any. Other than that, with one or two exceptions (fines, civil penalties, debts resulting from fraud, maintenance payments) you are freed from your debts.

The initial period

The Official Receiver will want to obtain detailed information from you and it is most likely that you will receive a booklet of questions to complete and return to him, to be followed up by an interview at his office. It will then be decided whether or not to call a meeting of creditors to appoint a trustee. It is also in this initial period that the Official Receiver, or the trustee in bankruptcy, if one is appointed, will decide whether or not to:

- Close down your business.
- Claim something of yours to sell.
- Ask you to make regular monthly payments out of your income.

● Investigate aspects of your financial affairs more fully.

How will it affect my life, my work and my business?

Whether you are employed, unemployed or continuing in business, you are likely to want a bank account. There is nothing in bankruptcy law to stop you running an account, but you will probably need to 'shop around' to find a bank who will allow you to operate one with them. It is most likely that you will not be able to have a cheque book or a bank card with your account. You will be able to pay money into your account in the usual ways, but you will probably only be able to draw cash out over the counter.

It is a criminal offence to ask somebody to provide you with credit of £250 or more without telling them that you are bankrupt. It is also a criminal offence to be a director of a limited company, or to be directly, or indirectly, involved in the management of a limited company.

Depending on the details of your regular income and expenditure, you may be asked to make a regular payment into your bankruptcy out of your income. If you do not do as you have been asked, then an application can be made to court for an order for payments to be made directly into your bankruptcy by your employer. If you have surplus income available for the bankruptcy, it is not impossible that there will be a stage at which the Official Receiver, or your trustee, will contact your employer.

If the Official Receiver and trustee have not told you that you will have to stop your business, then much of what you have been doing may continue as before the bankruptcy. You may continue to use the business name which you were using when you became bankrupt, the name quoted in the bankruptcy order. If you wish to use a new business name, then all your business paperwork should show your old business name, because the law assumes that anybody who knows your old business name will then know that you are bankrupt.

You should remember to set aside all that you need after the bankruptcy for tax etc. During your bankruptcy any unexpected gifts, 'wins', inheritances etc., must be paid to the Official Receiver or your trustee in bankruptcy. In addition when you become bankrupt:

- A property lease will probably be forfeit.
- A business partnership is automatically terminated.
- You must cease to act as a trustee of a trust.
- You may, depending on the rules of the organisation, lose your professional membership if you are, for example, a solicitor or accountant, and thus lose your livelihood.
- You are disqualified from sitting as a member in central or local government.
- There are high costs, especially if a large amount of funds are likely to become available.
- Your bankrupt position is publicly advertised.
- All your debts become due and payable.

What can be taken from you?

The trustee can only claim what is yours. If there is something which is claimed by you and someone else jointly, then the trustee is likely to write to the other person and ask whether or not they wish to buy out your share of the item. This may be the best way forward if the other person can do so.

None of the following items can be taken from you in your bankruptcy:

- Tools, books, vehicles or other items of equipment which are necessary for use personally or in your employment or business.
- Clothing, bedding, furniture, household equipment and provisions necessary for satisfying the basic domestic needs of you and your family.

If it is not possible for someone to make an offer which will enable you to keep something, then the trustee will probably want to have it sold and receive your share of the money obtained. If the trustee wants to sell your home, but you do not want him to do so, he will need to obtain a court order for possession and sale. The general rule is that the court will not make an order for possession until one year after the appointment of a trustee.

After the initial period

If you cannot afford to make payments out of your income when the bankruptcy starts, then the Official Receiver, or the trustee in bankruptcy, will probably ask you to let his office know if you become able to afford payments out of your income later on. If your income increases so that you can afford to make payments into your bankruptcy, then your duty is to tell the Official Receiver, or trustee, and start to make regular monthly payments. Your payments will stop when you are discharged.

The end – 'Discharge'

Your bankruptcy will end before your discharge if the bankruptcy order is 'annulled' by a court order. This can happen if: your bankruptcy was the result of someone else's mistake; you have paid everything which has to be paid in the bankruptcy; you have proposed an IVA to your creditors and they have accepted your proposal. Otherwise you will be automatically discharged from bankruptcy exactly three years after the date you were made bankrupt – OR – if the debts in your bankruptcy were less than £20,000, you may be discharged exactly two years after the date of the bankruptcy order.

Special rules apply if you have been bankrupt previously, or if you are made criminally bankrupt. Despite your discharge, the bankruptcy will continue to have a claim on anything of value of yours for as long as may be necessary after the three years.

Present experience indicates that credit reference agencies retain information concerning your bankruptcy on their files for sixteen years after your discharge from bankruptcy.